Desperate Glory

The Story of World War I

Stories of Canada

Desperate Glory

The Story of World War I

by

John Wilson

Series Editor: Allister Thompson

Napoleon Publishing

Napoleon Publishing
an imprint of Napoleon & Company
Toronto, Ontario, Canada
napoleonandcompany.com

Canadä

Le Conseil des Arts | The Canada Council
du Canada | for the Arts

Napoleon & Company acknowledges the support of the Canada Council
for our publishing program.

We acknowledge the financial support of
the Government of Canada through the Book Publishing Industry Development Program
(BPIDP) for our publishing activities.

Printed in Canada

Library and Archives Canada Cataloguing in Publication

Wilson, John (John Alexander), 1951-
        Desperate glory : the story of World War One / John Wilson.

Includes bibliographical references and index.

2nd printing September 2008
paperback ISBN 978-1-894917-81-0

        1. World War, 1914-1918--Juvenile literature. 2. World War,
1914-1918--Canada--Juvenile literature. 3. Canada--History--
1914-1918--Juvenile literature. 4. World War,--1914-1918--
Pictorial works. 5. World War, 1914-1918--Canada--
Pictorial works. 6. Canada--History--1914-1918—Pictorial
works. I. Title. II. Title: Story of World War One.
D522.7.W45 2008   j940.3'71   C2008-900043-9

In Memory of Private S/14143, Richard Symons Hay,
7th Battalion Queen's Own Cameron Highlanders.
Died 25th September, 1915, Loos, France.

Maps in this book:

An Awful Silence

In January 2000, a pair of tourists stumbled across some human bones in a field in a quiet corner of northern France. They turned out to belong to a Canadian soldier, Private David John Carlson. Private Carlson was one of the 60,383 Canadian soldiers who died in the First World War, and his body had remained lost for eighty-four years. Private Carlson was finally laid to rest with full military honours, but the war is still killing people today.

At eleven o'clock on Tuesday the 11th of November, 1919, something extraordinary happened across the British Empire. In Toronto, Melbourne, Auckland, London and thousands of other cities, towns and villages, the bustle ceased, traffic halted, factories shut down and trains stopped in mid-journey. In Nottingham, England, a murder trial hesitated—the judge, the lawyers and the accused man stood quietly. Then the trial continued, and the man was found guilty and condemned to death. For one hundred and twenty seconds, an eerie silence prevailed throughout the world's largest empire.

It was the first Armistice Day, or Remembrance Day, as we call it now, and it marked exactly one year since the end of the Great War, now called the First World War. But the silent people around the world weren't celebrating peace, they were remembering the dead—so many that, if only the British Empire casualties were to come to life and march four abreast past the Cenotaph monument in London, it would take three and a half days for them all to pass.

Nine million people—more than the entire population of Canada in 1914—died in the First World War, the map of Europe changed dramatically and the seeds were sown for an even more horrific war only twenty years later. The world of 1919 would never be the same as the world of 1914, and it all began with just two deaths on a warm summer's morning in a place few Canadians had ever heard of.

This seventeen-year-old Canadian soldier was wounded just fifteen minutes before the declaration of Armistice that ended the war.

The First Two Deaths

Princip and his fellow conspirators were members of Young Bosnia, a student group that believed that violence was the way to end Austrian rule and establish a greater Slavic state in the Balkans. They were helped by a shadowy Serbian organization called Black Hand which supplied weapons and smuggled assassins into Bosnia. The horrible irony of it all is that, in killing Franz Ferdinand, Princip eliminated the only important Austrian figure who supported greater freedom for the Bosnians.

Gavrilo Princip

On Sunday, June 28, 1914, on Franz Josef Street in downtown Sarajevo, the capital of Bosnia, a nineteen-year-old Serbian student, Gavrilo Princip, fired two shots at the heir to the Austrian throne and his wife. The first bullet went through the car door into Duchess Sophie's stomach, pushing her to the side and onto the floor. The second tore open Archduke Franz Ferdinand's neck, severing his jugular vein and spraying blood over the back seat of the car. As the pair died, Princip swallowed a cyanide capsule.

About an hour before Princip fired, one of his six colleagues had thrown a bomb at the archduke. It had missed but injured two army officers and some onlookers. Enraged at being an assassin's target, Franz Ferdinand had cancelled the day's activities—an army review and opening a local museum—and gone to visit the wounded officers. Unfortunately, no one told the driver, Franz Urban, of the change of plan, so he followed the original route. When the mistake was spotted, Urban was ordered to stop and reverse, immediately opposite the cafe where the despondent Princip sat, wondering what to do next. The assassin couldn't believe his luck. He stepped forward and fired the two shots that triggered the First World War.

There were only two deaths that day, because Princip's cyanide capsule didn't work. He was arrested, tried and thrown in prison, where he eventually died of tuberculosis as the war he had helped begin drew to a close.

The Archduke Franz Ferdinand, his wife
Sophie and their children

Archduke Franz Ferdinand and his wife Sophie died on their fourteenth wedding anniversary. He had taken her with him to visit Sarajevo because they didn't want to be apart on such an important day and because Sophie was pregnant with their fourth child.

Franz Ferdinand's death was significant because he was the only heir to the throne of the Austro-Hungarian Empire. Bosnia was a part of that empire and Serbia was not, although the Austrians wanted it to be. The old emperor, Franz Josef, used the assassination of his nephew as an excuse to threaten Serbia.

In Canada, few people paid much attention to these European squabbles on the far side of the Atlantic Ocean. It was a gloriously hot summer, and people were trying to cool off at the lake, where they might be reading the new novel by Edgar Rice Burroughs, *Tarzan of the Apes*, or, if they were stuck in the city, going to see Charlie Chaplin's latest antics in *Tillie's Punctured Romance*. They were excited by Sir Ernest Shackleton's attempt to cross Antarctica and much more worried about the possibility of civil war in Ireland, where many Canadian immigrants hailed from, than by the confusing events on the edges of Franz Josef's vast domain. They would soon be forced to pay a lot more attention.

ASSASSINAT DE L'ARCHIDUC HÉRITIER D'AUTRICHE
ET DE LA DUCHESSE SA FEMME A SARAJEVO

An illustration of the assassination
from a French magazine

Europe 1914

Norway

Sweden

Denmark

United Kingdom

Netherlands

Germany

Russia

Belgium

Luxembourg

France

Switzerland

Austro-Hungarian Empire

Italy

Bosnia
Sarajevo •

Romania

Spain

Montenegro

Serbia

Bulgaria

Albania

Greece

Ottoman Empire

800 kilometres

This map shows the political divisions of Europe as the war began in 1914.
See page 76 for a map showing the new face of Europe after the Treaty of Versailles in 1919.

A Hideous Inevitability

Franz Ferdinand's assassination began the slide to war, but railway timetables made the war inescapable.

On July 28th, the vast Austro-Hungarian Empire declared war on tiny Serbia. It was largely a bluff, to get what they wanted by threat. Russia, Serbia's protector, countered by announcing the mobilization of its huge army on July 30th. Russia's move was also mostly a bluff, but Germany now had a serious problem.

Germany was committed to helping Austria-Hungary against Russia, but France had a treaty with Russia—now Germany had enemies on both sides. The Germans couldn't fight both at once, but they had a plan. The German armies would attack France first and defeat it before Russia could be ready. It was a good plan—if Germany acted quickly—but Russia was already mobilizing.

Up to this point, it could all have been stopped, but as soon as Germany mobilized against France, the railway timetables took control. The railways were geared to transport millions of soldiers to the French border. It was a wonderfully efficient system, but it could only work in one direction. The railways were so crammed with trains going in one direction that, if they tried to turn around, chaos would erupt and the system feeding the troops onto the trains would collapse. The delay in sorting it all out would leave Germany defenceless while its enemies mobilized. On August 1st, the trains began moving west.

The German declaration of war, August 1, 1914

Von Schlieffen's Plan

Canada had no obvious role to play in all of this, but it was a dominion in the British Empire. As dominions, Canada and Newfoundland were largely independent, but had no control over their relations with other countries. Thus, Britain's declaration of war against Germany committed Canada and the other dominions to the war as well. Most people in Canada thought the war would be finished before they could get over to Europe, but like so many people in that far-off summer, they were horribly wrong.

The German plan was named after its creator, General von Schlieffen. The idea was that, once the soldiers got off the trains, they would march through neutral Belgium and attack France where there were no strong fortifications. In a huge arc, the armies would wheel around, capture Paris and attack the French armies in the rear. It would all be over in six weeks, and Germany could then concentrate on defeating Russia.

Great Britain declared war on Germany on August 4, 1914. Britain didn't go to war because it was attacked, but because its government didn't want to see Germany dominate Europe and because it wanted to defend Belgium's neutrality when the German soldiers invaded.

General Alfred Graf von Schlieffen

First Moves

The German plan was to walk from the Belgian border to Paris, just as the French plan was to walk from the German border to Berlin. They had no choice, since motor vehicles were few and unreliable. An army in 1914 moved on its feet at a slow walk. Everything it needed—from its artillery and ammunition to its food and medical supplies—was brought along by horses.

True, in the early days of August, trains carried armies around Europe much faster than in any previous war, but as soon as a soldier stepped onto a railway platform, he moved no faster than one of Napoleon's Old Guard or Julius Caesar's legionaries.

This meant that, throughout the war, it was possible to move reinforcements behind the lines much faster than an army could advance. This was one of the major causes of the trench stalemate.

Both France and Germany had vast armies in 1914, and the generals of both countries believed that the spirit and enthusiasm of their soldiers would win them battles. Unfortunately, spirit and enthusiasm do not do well against concentrated artillery and machine guns, and hundreds of thousands of men on both sides were mown down as they swarmed across open fields in the early Battles of the Frontiers.

The French army, in their splendid blue coats and red trousers, made inviting targets as they tried in vain to break through the German fortifications along their border. The Germans, in their less gaudy field grey uniforms, did better as they plodded in dense masses through Belgium and into northern France—until they reached the River Marne.

Here, the French and tiny British armies counterattacked and pushed the Germans away from Paris and toward the channel coast. It became a race as each army attempted to get around the end of the other. It was a race that no one won.

German soldiers at the Battle of the Marne, 1914

Enthusiasm

Conscription means that you do not have a choice about joining the army. In France and Germany before the war, every young man had to spend some time in the army. After he had served for a year or two, he had to spend a couple of weeks each year training. Thus, there were millions of trained men in Europe in 1914.

Britain and Canada did not need huge armies—Britain was protected by its navy, and Canada was a long way from Europe—so they had no conscription at the beginning of the war.

Being an island country with a strong navy, Britain did not need a huge conscript army like France, Germany and Russia. When war broke out, it sent its small but very well-trained army, the British Expeditionary Force, over to France then called for volunteers.

The response was extraordinary. In five months, over a million men volunteered. They joined for many reasons: for patriotism; because friends were joining up; to earn some money; because they were ashamed at being left behind; or simply for the adventure. Many thought the war would be over by Christmas. None of them had the faintest idea of the horrors they would experience.

A Canadian enlistment poster. Governments used such posters to try to convince men to sign up.

LANGEMARCKE
ST JULIEN
FESTUBERT
GIVENCHY

New names in Canadian history.
More are coming—
Will you be there?

ENLIST!

CJ Patterson

The Canadian Response

Robert Laird Borden was Canada's eighth Prime Minister. A teacher and lawyer from Nova Scotia, he was in office from 1911 to 1920. As well as overseeing Canada's involvement in the First World War, he did a lot to achieve recognition for Canada as an independent member of the British Commonwealth rather than just another part of the Empire. He also introduced income tax to Canada as a temporary measure to raise money to finance the war.

The response was enthusiastic throughout the British Empire. In Canada, a first contingent of 33,000 men sailed for Britain on October 3rd. But the situation was not as simple as it seemed. Of those 33,000, most had been born in Britain and had been in Canada only a few years. Most still regarded England as home, and only a thousand of the first volunteers were French Canadians. Nobody paid too much attention to this in the excitement of the moment, but it was to become more of a problem as the war dragged on.

Defence Minister Sam Hughes refused to allow Quebec volunteers to form their own units, and the men were spread through the English-speaking units, a policy that caused much bad feeling.

Prime Minister Robert Borden promised 500,000 volunteers from Canada's population of only eight million. By 1916, only 300,000 men had volunteered in Canada, and the enthusiasm of 1914 had vanished. Borden thought the time had come to force Canadians to fight in the war.

The Governor General, The Duke of Connaught, inspects Montreal Volunteers as they prepare to depart for Europe, 1915.

Battle and Retreat

A depiction of "The Angels of Mons" by British artist Alfred Pearce

---

There is a legend that at the height of the Battle of Mons, when the outnumbered British were being hardest pressed, a shimmering white angel appeared over the battlefield. Heartened, the tired soldiers fought on.

Or maybe it was a ghostly army of bowmen fighting beside them. Most likely, nothing happened at all. No diary or letter about the battle mentions any supernatural occurrence, but miracles die hard, and the "Angel of Mons" is still recorded in some modern histories.

People in Britain wanted to believe that God was on their side in the confusion of war, in the same way that many today believe in "urban myths".

The 70,000 men of the British Expeditionary Force (BEF) marched into Belgium and, on August 22nd, dug a line of shallow trenches on either side of the coal mining town of Mons. At around ten the next morning, as the mist cleared, the men of the BEF saw masses of German infantry leave the woods in front of them and swarm forward.

The BEF was outnumbered by more than three to one, but they had a skill that surprised the Germans. During the Boer War in South Africa, they had learned how to use cover, and each man was trained to fire his rifle fifteen times a minute. At around 1000 yards range, they opened fire, and the German infantry fell in heaps.

Throughout the day, the Germans kept attacking, losing almost 10,000 men in the process. But it was not completely one-sided. The British lost around 3,000 men, and by evening were being threatened with encirclement. The next day, leaving the ground in front of their trenches littered with German dead and wounded, the British retreated.

Mons marked the beginning of the war for the BEF. More than four years later, the same town marked the end of the war for the Canadians who liberated it on the final day of fighting.

Tannenberg and Ypres

German soldiers at Tannenberg

At the same time that the British were retreating from Mons, in a forest outside the village of Tannenberg, close to the Russian border with Germany, Russian general Samsonov, alone and desperate, put a gun to his head and killed himself. He had just lost the greatest battle of the war so far, and he could not face the shame.

Germany had been surprised by how quickly Russia had mobilized and sent two armies to invade East Prussia. But the armies were poorly led and equipped. The Germans defeated one at Tannenberg and forced the other to retreat. It was a disaster for Russia, but it had one unexpected benefit for the Allies. Worried by the Russian advance, the Germans had sent three army corps from France to help. They arrived too late, but their absence fatally weakened von Schlieffen's plan to overcome France quickly.

The German army never reached Paris. Missing the troops sent east and exhausted by weeks of marching, it swung south to the Marne River. There the

In 1914, the major Allies, bound together by treaties, were Russia, Britain and France. Against them were the Central Powers of Germany and the Austro-Hungarian Empire.

As the war went on, others were drawn in, Turkey on the side of the Central Powers, and Japan, Romania, Bulgaria and Italy on the side of the Allies. In 1917 the United States joined the Allies and was followed by China, Brazil and many other South American countries. It had truly become a global war.

The location of the battle of Tannenberg.

Allies attacked from the south and from Paris. Some soldiers were carried to war in taxicabs. They halted the German advance and began pushing them back. The race north ended at a small Belgian town whose name was to become synonymous with horror—Ypres.

At the end of October, the British army faced overwhelming odds around Ypres. For more than three weeks, they were almost continuously attacked by massed ranks of German infantry. At one point, only a scratch force of cooks and clerks stood between the German army and Ypres itself. The Germans were slaughtered in their thousands, but it wasn't one-sided. By mid-November, when the battle petered out, and the survivors dug trenches to protect them for the winter, the British regular army that had marched so cheerfully to Mons was only a fraction of its former size. There would be many more battles, some much bloodier than this First Ypres, but the fighting would be by the men who had flocked to volunteer from London, Glasgow, Auckland, Sydney, St. John's, Toronto and Winnipeg.

A ruined cathedral in Ypres. No buildings, not even churches, were spared the fury of artillery fire.

12

Truce

An incredible event occurred during the first Christmas of the war. Hundreds of thousands of soldiers had died, and the war in France had stagnated into a line of trenches that ran for almost 700 kilometres from the English Channel to the Swiss border. Soldiers on both sides watched each other from their trenches across a barren stretch of ground called "no man's land", that varied from a kilometre to a few tens of metres wide. If a soldier poked his head above the trench, he was sure to be shot at.

For most of December 1914, it rained over Northern France, but late on Christmas Eve, the skies cleared and the ground froze. As darkness fell, all along the front, British and French soldiers were amazed to see small, candlelit Christmas trees appear along the German trenches. Then the singing began—"Silent Night" and "O Tannenbaum" from the Germans, "Good King Wenceslas" and soldiers' songs from the British.

The next day, the guns were silent. Somewhere, a soldier stood up. No one shot at him. Soon thousands of men from both sides were meeting each other in no man's land. Cigarettes, food, brandy and schnapps were exchanged.

Sentry duty at the front, 1916

Enemy soldiers met briefly
as brothers during
the Christmas Truce.

Photographs of loved ones back home were admired. A soldier of the Argyll and Sutherland Highlanders produced a football. Caps and helmets were put down to mark goals, and a soccer match was played against the Germans—the 133rd Saxon Regiment. The Saxons won by three goals to two.

For a day, enemies became human, and the war stopped. Men who hours before had been busily trying to kill each other chatted and joked in the open. But the miracle of the Christmas truce couldn't last. The generals disapproved and ordered the guns to fire again. In most places on Boxing Day, the war went on as usual. The Christmas truce of 1914 was never repeated, but it remains a bright spot of sanity amid the madness of war.

Stalemate

Hannibal was a Carthaginian general who lived from 247 to 183 BCE. He is famous for taking elephants across the Alps to fight against the Romans in Italy, where he won many startling victories. He was finally defeated in North Africa at the battle of Zama.

Napoleon Bonaparte rose to power during the French Revolution and his armies defeated everyone in Europe. He was eventually beaten by the Duke of Wellington at Waterloo in 1815.

Robert E. Lee led the armies of the South in the American Civil War. Lee was a much cleverer general than his opponents in the North, and for years won many stunning victories. However, the North

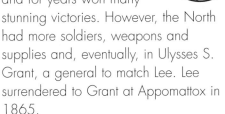

had more soldiers, weapons and supplies and, eventually, in Ulysses S. Grant, a general to match Lee. Lee surrendered to Grant at Appomattox in 1865.

Many battles before 1914 were won by a stroke of genius. A brilliant general like Hannibal, Napoleon or Robert E. Lee, could surprise an enemy, outflank him or draw him into a place where he was at a disadvantage. By 1915, this was no longer possible for the generals of the British, French and German armies.

The apparently endless trenches facing each other across no man's land fixed the armies in place and did not allow for any brilliant moves. To win, a general had to make his army fight through the enemy lines. How to do this occupied the best military minds of three nations for almost four years.

The reason it took so long and cost so many soldiers' lives was that the technology of 1914—artillery, bombs and machine guns—favoured defending a position, while the technology that would allow the attacker to win—tanks, bombers and wireless radios—had not yet been developed.

The generals in the First World War seem stupid today because they fought huge battles that cost hundreds of thousands of lives and only advanced their army a kilometre or two. Serious mistakes were made, and generals learned painfully slowly from their mistakes, but they were often trapped by the technology of their time. It is unlikely that famous generals of the past would have fared much better in this war.

Canadian artillerymen

A New Year Looms

Nineteen-fourteen had not turned out as anyone expected. The war of movement with huge armies marching and fighting traditional battles had only lasted three months and had cost hundreds of thousands of lives. The continuous trenches were only two months old by Christmas, and the Allies still had high hopes that a major attack would break through the enemy lines and restore a war of movement.

For Germany, the Schlieffen plan hadn't worked, but the Germans still had the upper hand, having beaten the Russian offensive and taken large areas of Belgium and France.

The Austro-Hungarian Empire had not won the easy victory over Serbia they had gone to war to achieve. Russia had attacked and had been defeated, but it still had a huge army that could threaten the German and Austrian borders.

The French plan to march on Berlin had also failed, but now they had a strong focus, to force the Germans back out of their territory.

The British regular army had been badly mauled. It was obvious that, if Britain was to contribute, it would need to turn the million enthusiastic volunteers into soldiers as quickly as possible. Canada was not yet involved, but the 33,000 men of the First Canadian Division were in Europe being trained to go into battle.

Although the war only began in August, 1914 was one of the bloodiest years. Although records are not precise, the French probably lost more men in the five months of 1914 than in any other full year of the war. This was because the early battles were fought by masses of men in the open, in the French case dressed in bright red and blue uniforms. As the British found at Mons, crowded men in open fields provided an unmissable target for rifles, machine guns and artillery.

Ypres Again

The gas used at Second Ypres was chlorine, which attacked the lungs and caused the victim to drown. A nurse described a dying Canadian soldier after the first attack: "He was sitting on the bed, fighting for breath, his lips plum coloured. He was a magnificent young Canadian past all hope in the asphyxia of chlorine. I shall never forget the look in his eyes as he turned to me and gasped: 'I can't die! Is it possible that nothing can be done for me?'"

The first British attempt to break the stalemate was at Neuve Chapelle on March 10, 1915. It failed at the cost of 13,000 dead and wounded. The following month, the Germans tried using a new weapon.

Late on the afternoon of April 22, French units outside Ypres noticed a greenish cloud moving toward them across no man's land. As the cloud engulfed the soldiers, they began coughing, choking and dying. A division fled, leaving a large hole in the line, but the Germans were unprepared for their success and could not exploit it.

The following day, another cloud descended on the first Canadian soldiers to arrive in France. The Canadians were overrun but defended bravely, and machine gunner Fred Fisher became the first Canadian soldier in the First World War to be awarded the Victoria Cross, Britain's highest award for gallantry.

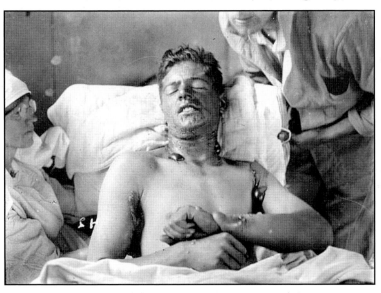

A Canadian soldier suffering from the effects of mustard gas

Both sides used poison gas in World War I, but the British and French always had the advantage because the prevailing winds in northern France for most of the year are from west to east. Although Ypres in 1915 marked the first concentrated use of poison gas, the French had tried it as early as 1914, and the Germans had been experimenting against Russian soldiers. Poison gas was not used extensively in World War II, but some 20,000 Iranian soldiers and an unknown number of civilians were killed by Iraqi gas attacks during the Iran-Iraq war of 1980 to 1988.

The battle dragged on until the middle of May, but Second Ypres will always be remembered as the first use in the war of poison gas.

The British and Canadians were quick to develop and introduce primitive but effective gas masks, and the soldiers discovered that if they urinated on a gauze pad and held it to their noses, the ammonia in the urine neutralized the chlorine. Throughout the war, the Germans developed and tried different kinds of poison gas. Each time a new gas was introduced, the Allies quickly developed an effective mask then began using the gas themselves.

Initially, the problem with gas was that it required a favourable wind to blow it toward the enemy and, sometimes, the wind changed and blew the gas back on the attackers. Gas shells were more effective, but poison gas never turned out to be the war-winning weapon the Germans had hoped for.

Soldiers wearing gas masks to protect their eyes and lungs

Somewhere Else

Winston Churchill, the son of a famous British politician, fought in India and the Sudan at the end of the nineteenth century. After becoming a politician himself, as First Lord of the Admiralty in the British Government at the beginning of the war, Churchill was energetic in supporting new ideas, such as the tank and the landings at Gallipoli.

He later became one of the most famous people of the twentieth century by leading Britain as prime minister during the Second World War, making stirring speeches on the radio and inspiring the British people's resolve to resist German bombings.

Canadian Prime Minister Borden (left) with Winston Churchill in 1912

As the casualties mounted in France, and no one could see a way to break through the enemy trenches, some people began looking for alternative ways to win the war. One idea, supported by Winston Churchill, was to attack Germany's ally, Turkey, at Gallipoli, capture their capital, Constantinople (today's Istanbul), and force them out of the war. With Turkey defeated, the Dardanelles, the strait from the Mediterranean Sea to the Black Sea, would be open and allow Britain and France to support Russia by putting pressure on Germany from the east.

The first plan was for the British and French navies to force a way through the Dardanelles. When this failed, and three Allied battleships were sunk by mines on March 18, it was decided to take the Gallipoli Peninsula by landing soldiers on the beaches. Allied soldiers from Australia and New Zealand came ashore on five separate beaches at dawn on April 25th, 1915. Three landings, S, X and Y beaches, were only lightly opposed, but two, V and W beaches, were hotly contested.

At V Beach, an old ship, the *River Clyde,* was driven ashore, and the men let down ramps. They were mowed down by Turkish machine guns. At W Beach, the boats being rowed ashore were hit by machine gun and rifle fire, and the equipment-laden men who jumped into the water sank and drowned. More than half the 3,000 men on V and W beaches were killed or wounded that day.

The soldiers at Gallipoli succeeded in fighting their way off the beaches but failed to take the heights on the peninsula or to threaten the Turkish guns that dominated the Dardanelles. Both sides dug trenches, and the campaign became a miniature version of the Western Front. For eight months, the casualties rose with no appreciable change in the lines on the map. Finally, in December 1915 and January 1916, in the only successful operation of the whole misguided campaign, the entire Allied force was evacuated without a single casualty.

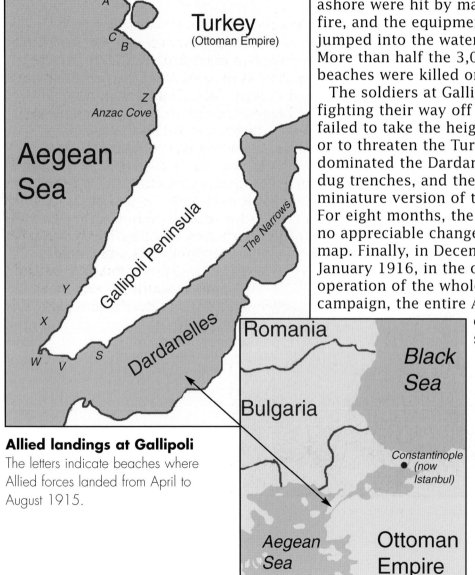

Allied landings at Gallipoli
The letters indicate beaches where Allied forces landed from April to August 1915.

The Australian Experience

In 1914, Canada, Newfoundland, Australia and New Zealand were all dominions in the British empire.

Despite being nations with some independence, many Canadians, Newfoundlanders, Australians and New Zealanders regarded themselves as British. The profile of these countries was raised during the war, and the sacrifices of their soldiers gave the populations of the dominions a new sense of pride in their own countries.

No Canadian units fought at Gallipoli, but the peninsula became synonymous with a new sense of nationhood for two other British colonies. In the predawn darkness of April 25th, the Australian and New Zealand Corps (ANZAC) landed north of Z beach and below a bewilderingly rugged landscape of cliffs, steep ridges and gullies.

Through the blistering heat of summer and the bitter cold of winter, the ANZACs fought and died in this barren landscape thousands of miles from home. Their exploits became legend at home and, although they failed to take Gallipoli, they gave their countries a sense of identity. The beach on which the first of them landed is still called ANZAC Cove. Australians and New Zealanders remember their war dead every year on April 25th.

The Anzac landing

Sideshows

In the early days of the war, the Germans used several light cruisers to attack British shipping around the world. The most successful was the SMS *Emden*.

Operating in the Indian Ocean between September and November, 1914, the *Emden* sank eighteen merchant ships, a Russian cruiser and a French destroyer. It also captured three colliers and shelled Madras and Penang. The crew of the *Emden* was noted for its gentlemanly conduct, and not one crew member from the sunk merchantmen was killed, all being released to neutral ships.

At last, the *Emden* was cornered by the Australian cruiser HMAS *Sydney*. After suffering more than a hundred direct hits, the *Emden* surrendered. However, the forty men of the crew commandeered a schooner, *Ayesha*, and after an epic voyage, they arrived in Turkey in 1915.

While the huge armies of Germany, Austria-Hungary, Russia, France and Britain fought in massive, bloody battles in Europe, or tried to find alternatives in Gallipoli, a dozen minor but no less brutal campaigns were being fought across the world.

In 1914, Germany had an empire of African and Pacific island colonies. When war broke out, the Pacific islands were taken over quickly, and the four African colonies—Togoland, Cameroon, German South-West Africa (Namibia) and German East Africa (Tanzania)—were surrounded by Allied colonies. The first three fell to the Allies by 1915, but German East Africa was harder to take.

The commander of the small German army in East Africa was Colonel von Lettow-Vorbeck, and for four years, he conducted a successful campaign, tying up British resources and supplies, making raids into neighbouring Kenya, Uganda and Mozambique and even creating a tiny navy on Lake Victoria. So successful was von Lettow-Vorbeck that he didn't surrender until November 23, 1918, twelve days after the war in Europe ended.

At the end of the war, the old German colonies were divided amongst the victorious nations.

The damaged *Emden*

Trying Again

A connection to the author
When the war broke out, teenager Richard Symons Hay left his home in Ayr on the west coast of Scotland, lied about his age and became private soldier number S/14143 of the 7th Battalion, Queen's Own Cameron Highlanders. He was trained and given a new uniform, complete with kilt, and sent over to France. Late on the morning of September 25th, when the rest of the 15th Scottish Division was in trouble on Hill 70, Richard's battalion of around 750 soldiers was sent in to help. They came under heavy German shellfire and, over the next few days, 687 were either killed or wounded. Richard was one of the dead on the first day, either directly hit by a shell or buried, and his body was never found.

All that remains today to mark Richard's life is his name, carved on the Loos Memorial to the missing at Dud Corner Cemetery, and a photograph of him, taken in Glasgow in 1915, showing him standing proudly on the right in his new uniform. That photograph hangs on my living room wall, because Richard Symons Hay was my wife's great-uncle.

By the fall of 1915, many of the British volunteers from the previous year were ready for battle. It was decided to attack the German lines around the coal-mining town of Loos in France, a difficult landscape of mine tips, mine head-frames and small villages of miners' cottages. The attack was planned for September 25th and, for the first time, the British would use poison gas to support their 75,000 attackers.

The day began badly for the British. In many places, the wind was too weak to blow the gas, and in some cases it even blew back on the British soldiers. However, the 15th Scottish Division broke through the German lines, taking the town of Loos and advancing up Hill 70. But as the soldiers swept down the far side of the hill, they were caught in intense machine gun and artillery fire from the German second line of trenches, and the attack was halted.

On the following day, the attacks were renewed again—and again and again on subsequent days. Eventually, on October 14th, after 8,000 Allied men had been killed and 50,000 wounded, the offensive was called off with no appreciable gains. Almost 7,000 of the Allied casualties were from the 15th Scottish Division.

In 1915, the trenches in France were in the same place they had been twelve months before, but now they were much stronger, and the Allied attempt to go around them through Gallipolli had failed miserably. The Germans had taken a lot of Russian territory but had failed to knock them out of the war. Austria-Hungary had finally taken Serbia, but its army was not doing well and needed support from its German allies. Britain now had a much larger army, but most of the volunteers were untried in battle. Canadians had fought, but they were still not a major force.

On both sides of the trenches, much had been learned. The Germans knew how to strengthen their defences. New inventions, like poison gas and aircraft, were playing a role but were not decisive weapons. It looked as though 1916 would follow the pattern of the previous year.

The Other Side of Europe

While the British and French were struggling to break the deadlock on the Western Front, the Germans had transferred the bulk of their army to the east in an attempt to win the war there.

In the east, the distances were so great that it was impossible to build and man a continuous trench line, so the war there was much more fluid. Throughout 1915, the German and Austro-Hungarian armies relentlessly pushed the Russians out of Poland and large areas of Western Russia. They took Warsaw, Poland's capital, on August 4th but, despite invading huge tracts of land and capturing or killing hundreds of thousands of Russian soldiers, they failed to force Russia out of the war.

The Austro-Hungarian armies had more luck in finally getting revenge for the assassination of Franz Ferdinand. In October and November, with German and Bulgarian help, they invaded Serbia and forced the army and the king to flee.

In April 1915, Italy agreed to join Britain and France. The following month, they attacked the Austro-Hungarian army on the Isonzo River but failed to get anywhere and suffered 300,000 casualties before the offensive was called off in the fall. Much of the fighting between Italy and Austria-Hungary took place among the soaring peaks of the Alps.

Russian soldiers in Warsaw, Poland, 1914

War in the Third Dimension

German Fokker triplanes

In August 1914, few people thought that airplanes would be important in the war. In fact, Marshal Ferdinand Foch of the French Army said, "The aircraft is all very well for sport—for the army it is useless." But things changed rapidly.

At first, airplanes were only used for observation—it was from a plane that the swing of the German Army away from Paris in September 1914 was noticed—but pilots soon began to try and bring each other down. At first, this was done

with pistols or rifles, or even by dropping sharp metal darts on the opponent. Pilots were at greater risk from their own flimsy machines than from enemy action. However, Major Lanoe G. Hawker mounted a machine gun to fire at an angle so that he missed his own propeller, and on July 25th, 1915 became the first Victoria Cross winner in the air for downing three enemy planes.

A machine gun mounted to fire at enemy planes

The air aces of the war were seen by the public on both sides as heroes. They fought in individual combat in the clean air above the mud and death of the trenches, and the newspapers often compared them to medieval knights dueling on horseback. Richthofen, known as the Red Baron, and the others became household names, and they were given huge public funerals when they died. The reality was a bit different. Richthofen was a cold-blooded killer who attacked few of his eighty kills unless he had an overwhelming advantage.

Most of his victims were slow, poorly armed spotter planes that stood little chance against his fast, heavily-armed, bright red triplane (a plane with three wings). And the victims never died cleanly. They either fell to their deaths from hundreds of feet, or burned to death, trapped in their wood and canvas machines. The British ace, Mick Mannock, had such fear of his aircraft catching fire that he carried a revolver with him so he could shoot himself rather than burn. The war in the air was different from the trenches, but it was still war.

Pilots who had shot down many enemy planes were called "aces". Sixteen months later, Hawker was killed in an air duel with German "ace" Manfred von Richthofen.

As the technology improved, air warfare became more deadly. The 1915 German introduction of a machine gun that could fire directly ahead through the spinning propellor gave them an advantage that they held until the following year. During this time, Max Immelman and Oswald Boelcke developed the principles of air combat, became the first German "aces" with eight victories each and were hailed by the newspapers as heroes. Both died in the air in 1916.

Manfred von Richthofen,
the "Red Baron"

Flying Canadians

With no air force of their own, Canadian flyers joined the Royal Flying Corps (RFC) of the British Army or the Royal Naval Air Service (RNAS). Despite often being considered not suitable material by the elitist British—one man was rejected because he was a farm labourer, another because he owned a newspaper stand in Regina—thirty-seven Canadian airmen enlisted in 1915, a figure that rose to 905 in 1916 and 7782 in the last year of the war.

Canadian "ace" William Barker poses with a downed German airplane.

Aces like Richthofen and Hawker were the public heroes of the war. More vital were the observers in the slow spotter planes that Richthofen preyed on. They were the men who, while their pilot flew slowly in straight lines over the battlefield, had to concentrate on taking photographs of the enemy trenches or spotting enemy guns. They were the eyes of the modern army, and the dogfights that so thrilled civilians at home only occurred so that these men could do their job.

One of the most colourful early Canadian volunteers in the RFC was Stanley Cawes, who had a habit of hurling knives into the wooden doors of the mess room. On September 21st, 1915, Cawes and his observer were attacked by several German planes. After a long fight, Cawes was shot and killed, becoming the first Canadian casualty of the war in the air. His observer was wounded and captured.

Hanging on

Stories of Verdun became legend in France. The road to the town, along which supplies for the beleaguered French army had to go, was called the Sacred Way; a pigeon that carried the last message out of a doomed French fort was given a medal; and a squad of soldiers was buried in a trench by shellfire, with only the bayonets of their rifles sticking up above ground.

Today, the ruined forts can still be seen, as can huge memorials to the dead. Visitors are warned not to leave the paths because the woods around are still filled with unexploded ammunition.

French troops in a muddy trench at Verdun

(above) The grisly reality of war: the remains of German soldiers at Verdun

Despite the failures of 1915, the Allies began 1916 hopefully. Britain's volunteer army was finally ready, and the joint offensive to end the war was planned for the spring. It never got started.

At 7:15 on the morning of February 21st, 1916, Germany launched its only major offensive on the Western Front between 1914 and 1918. After an intense artillery bombardment that rained 100,000 shells per hour on the French defences, an army of a million men attacked over a twelve kilometre front. Their object was the town of Verdun, but to get there they had to get past a series of forts that guarded the approaches.

In fact, the Germans didn't intend to take Verdun. They wanted to draw the French Army into a battle of attrition and destroy it—to "bleed France white" as the German commander, Erich von Falkenhayn, put it. They almost did. The battle, which slowed by July but stuttered on until December, cost France 550,000 casualties. But 434,000 German soldiers were killed or wounded too.

Verdun achieved nothing for either France or Germany except unimaginable suffering and the weakening of both armies. For Britain and Canada, the consequences were equally bloody, but not in the mud around Verdun. For the volunteers of 1914, Verdun led them, later that summer, north to the banks of the Somme River, where another great battle awaited them.

Canaries

Although all the soldiers in the First World War were men, women played important roles. Close to the battlefields, they staffed the aid posts and hospitals as nurses and orderlies. Many wounded soldiers survived because of the care and attention of these women.

At home, women began to take over jobs in factories as men went overseas to fight. This had never been done before, and many people thought it was wrong for women to work, or that they wouldn't be able to do the jobs. Thousands of women proved them wrong. Unfortunately, they were almost all let go from their jobs when the men returned in 1918 and 1919.

One place where women were particularly prized was in the munitions factories. It was said that their small hands helped with the delicate work on the fuses of shells. The girls who worked in the munitions factories were called Canary Girls because the explosives they worked with turned their skin a bright yellow colour.

Female munitions workers in Montreal, 1916

Canadian munitions factories produced one million shells per month, and other factories built submarines and supplied aircraft parts. Much of the work was done by women, and it had far-reaching effects.

Several countries, including Australia and New Zealand, had given women the vote before the war started. In Canada, the war work done by women sped up the process. Manitoba led the way by allowing women to vote in 1916, and most provinces and the federal government followed suit. Quebec allowed women to vote in 1940.

Daddy, what did *YOU* do in the Great War?

Posters like this one were used to try to convince men to sign up with the armed services.

It was also dangerous work. On July 1st, 1918, the munitions factory at Chilwell near Nottingham in England, that had supplied most of the shells for the Somme, exploded, killing 134 workers. The cause was never determined, but the explosion could be heard thirty miles away. Rumours of sabotage persisted for long afterwards.

Women also performed another, less heroic role, at home. Any man of military age not in uniform was likely to be handed a white feather by a woman. This was a symbol of cowardice, suggesting that the man was too frightened to join the army. The feathers angered soldiers home on leave and out of uniform, but no one knows how many young men were shamed into joining the army and eventually being killed in the war.

Women contributed a great deal to the war in ways other than fighting. Recognition of their contribution helped women get the vote in many places after the war was over.

Troubles In Britain

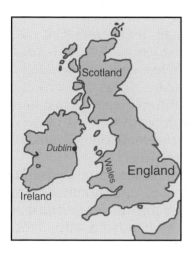

While most of the British Army was preparing for the summer battles of 1916, some of their colleagues were engaged much closer to home—in the streets of Dublin.

Ireland had been struggling for some form of independence from Britain for many years, and there had been numerous armed rebellions. In the summer of 1914, many people thought that the major threat of war was not in Europe, but of civil war in Ireland. Although thousands of Irishmen volunteered to fight in the British army, some leaders of the independence movement saw Britain's involvement in Europe as a golden opportunity. On April 24, Easter Monday, about 1,200 rebels, armed with weapons they had bought in secret from Germany, took over key buildings in Dublin, including the post office.

The rebels hoped that the British would offer Ireland independence rather than become involved in costly fighting away from France.

The aftermath: extensive damage to Dublin's general post office

In an odd little sideline, the main British firepower in the early days of the rebellion was provided by a gunboat, *Helga,* which fired many shells into Dublin. After Irish Independence in 1921, the *Helga* was bought by the Irish Free State and became the first vessel in the new nation's navy.

The war in Ireland that observers had feared finally erupted in 1919. It ended with Irish independence in 1921, although the bloodshed continued in civil war until 1923. The United Kingdom retained North Ireland, which has led to ongoing violence over the years until the present day.

However, the Easter Rising was badly planned, and when the British brought 16,000 troops and artillery into the city, it was doomed.

The fighting raged all week, and much of downtown Dublin was destroyed or damaged by shellfire, but by April 30 it was all over and the rebels surrendered. Sixty-four rebels and one hundred and fifty-seven soldiers died in the fighting. Caught in the middle, more than two hundred civilians were killed in the crossfire.

Many Irish people blamed the rebels for the civilian deaths and the destruction, but the harsh British reprisals—they hanged sixteen rebel leaders, one of whom was so badly wounded he had to be strapped to a chair to be killed—turned opinion against the British troops and increased support for independence.

The Irish rebels' proclamation of independence.

The Somme—Day 1

What went wrong on that dreadful morning? In a word, inexperience.

The generals were inexperienced in this type of war and in handling such large numbers of soldiers. The British artillerymen were inexperienced in destroying the German barbed wire, trenches and artillery, and the soldiers were inexperienced in performing complicated manoeuvers under enemy fire. Thus, the soldiers were trained to simply walk forward into intact enemy defences. Even where the soldiers succeeded, poor communications prevented the generals from finding out what was happening and sending support or exploiting the success.

Where local commanders used some imagination, such as sending their troops out into no man's land the night before so they could rush into the German trenches before the enemy were ready, or where the soldiers hurried forward under cover of smoke, the attacks of July 1st were successful, and many fewer Allied soldiers died.

At 7:30 a.m. on July 1st, 1916, a warm, sunny morning, whistles blew in the British trenches along the Somme River. Tens of thousands of young men, mostly the boys who had volunteered so enthusiastically almost two years before, clambered out of their trenches and walked forward over green fields scattered with red and yellow flowers. They walked slowly because they were each carrying more than thirty kilograms of equipment, but they arranged themselves in neat, straight lines.

The Germans on the other side of no man's land, clambering out of their dugouts or peering out of their concrete strong points, couldn't believe their eyes. The machine guns began clacking like loud, old-fashioned sewing machines, and men dropped, one by one, all along the neat lines. Shells began exploding and tearing holes in the rows. Those who survived this were shot as they tried to find a way through the German wire.

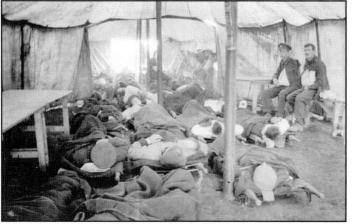

Wounded Canadian soldiers at the Somme

The British colony of Newfoundland rejected confederation with Canada in 1869. It became a dominion of the British Empire at the same time as New Zealand in 1907. In a pair of controversial and tightly fought referenda in 1948, Newfoundlanders voted narrowly for confederation and in 1949, Newfoundland and Labrador became Canada's tenth province.

It was the worst day in the history of the British Army. By sunset, almost 20,000 young men were lying dead among the summer flowers, and another 40,000 had been wounded.

At 9:05 that morning, in front of the village of Beaumont Hamel, 780 volunteers from Newfoundland, which was not a part of Canada back then, set off to cover the 900 metres between themselves and the German trenches. As the machine-guns opened fire, the men hunched forward as if "fighting their way home against a blizzard in some little outport in far off Newfoundland." Within half an hour, 698 of them were dead, dying or wounded.

Memorial University in St. John's, Newfoundland, is named in memory of the island's war dead.

The Rooms Provincial Archives, E 29-7/attributed to R.P. Holloway

Soldiers from Newfoundland and Labrador aboard ship and leaving St. John's to fight in the war, 1914

The Somme—
Day 2 to Day 141

Ruins at the village of Courcelette with a shell explosion in the background

The Battle of the Somme didn't end on July 1st. It continued for another four and a half months and cost a total of 415,000 British casualties, including 24,000 Canadians.

The battle didn't continue every day all along the front, but consisted of dozens of localized attacks and counter attacks. For example, on September 15th, the Canadians attacked near the village of Courcelette. They achieved their objectives because the artillery was effective, the soldiers didn't try to walk forward and the generals were trying new things—such as using tanks for the first time in battle.

German counterattacks and more British and Canadian attacks at Courcelette meant that the battle went on for weeks, and thousands of soldiers died, but lessons were very slowly being learned.

By November, winter had come, and the rain made it impossible to keep fighting.

At the end of the battle, the British and French had advanced eight kilometres at their farthest point, and, in many places, not even as far as they had hoped to advance on July 1st. It was a small gain at the cost of so many dead and wounded. Almost 600,000 German soldiers also became casualties, a cost from which the German army never recovered. One officer said that the Somme was the muddy graveyard of the German army. Although no one won the battle, if it had not been fought, it is doubtful that the Allies could have won the war when they did. Perhaps all those young men did not die in vain after all.

Jutland

The British battlecruisers tended to explode because their armour was not thick enough on top. Shells coming down on the ships could pierce the armor, explode and ignite the unstable cordite explosive in the ship's magazine, where the ammunition is kept.

During Jutland, the *Indefatigable*, *Invincible* and *Queen Mary* all blew up, killing 3,309 men. Only seventeen men survived from all three ships.

The *Lion* was saved from the same fate when a shell destroyed one of its gun turrets and fire raced toward the magazine. Despite having had his legs blown off, Major Francis John William Harvey of the Royal Marines stayed conscious long enough to order the magazine doors closed and the magazine flooded with sea water. The ship was saved, although Harvey died of his wounds.

Britain went to war with a tiny army and a huge navy. The army grew and fought numerous battles. The navy fought only one major engagement, on May 31st, 1916, as the army was preparing for the Somme.

For almost two years, the British Grand Fleet had controlled the seas, blockading German ports and forcing Germany's smaller High Seas Fleet to stay in port. But the Germans had a plan. They would send out their battlecruisers to lure a small number of British ships to their main fleet of battleships. Unfortunately for them, the British had broken the German navy code and knew of the trap.

In the middle of the afternoon, the British battlecruisers met the Germans at Jutland off the coast of Denmark, and a running battle began. The British suffered losses and, as the commander watched his ships explode, he commented, "There seems to be something wrong with our...ships today."

Ships of the British fleet at Jutland

The HMS *Lion* on fire

Admiral
John Jellicoe

By evening, the battleships were engaged, but darkness forced an end to the battle. The Germans ran for home and made it back to port safely. Neither fleet was destroyed. The British lost more ships, fourteen to the German eleven, but the German fleet never left port again.

The British had a lot more to lose in the battle than the Germans. If the German High Seas Fleet had been destroyed, the war would have gone on as before. If the British Grand Fleet had been sunk, the blockade of Germany would have been broken, and the Germans could have shelled British ports and stopped their soldiers being sent over to France. The British Admiral Sir John Jellicoe was so important to the war effort that he was called by future prime minister Winston Churchill, "the only man who could have lost the war in an afternoon".

The *Invincible* sinks to the bottom.

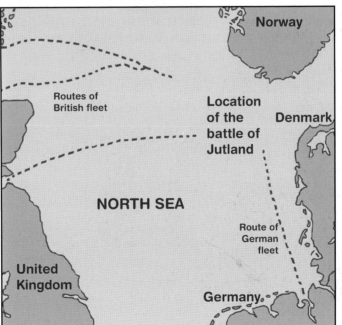

Norway

Routes of British fleet

Location of the battle of Jutland

Denmark

NORTH SEA

Route of German fleet

United Kingdom

Germany

Trench Life

While the soldiers were suffering and dying in the trenches, a very different war was going on in secret.

The invention of wireless telegraphy made it much easier for armies and navies to communicate. The drawback was that anyone with a receiver could listen in. Codes became vital.

When the western front sank into stalemate at the end of 1914, the Germans were on French and Belgium soil. Therefore they were happy to stay on the defensive and build trenches that were designed to be semi-permanent. They dug deep dugouts, built concrete strong points and tried to make their troops as secure as possible.

The French and British regarded their trenches as jumping-off points for the eventual attack that would drive the Germans back, so they built less permanent fortifications. Consequently, the Allied soldiers were much less comfortable than they could have been and were always amazed at the complexity and strength of the German trenches they captured.

However, all trenches had several things in common. The parapet was the trench wall that faced the enemy. It was usually deep enough that a man could walk behind it without his head sticking up. Because of this, it needed a firestep so that a soldier could fire his rifle over the top during an attack.

A Canadian trench with "funk holes", where the soldiers would take shelter and catch some rest

A Canadian communication trench with duckboards. Communication trenches were dug between the front and back lines of a position to provide protection when passing between them.

The back wall was called the parados and was usually lower than the parapet. In good trenches, wooden slats, called duckboards, lay along the trench floor to keep it dry. Dugouts were cut into the trench walls for the soldiers to sleep in. Sometimes these were only shallow pits, just wide enough for a man to lie down.

Trenches were never straight. Every few yards, there was a right-angled corner so that, from the air, they looked a bit like the battlements on a castle. Trenches were built this way to limit the effects of a shell exploding there or to stop an enemy firing his gun along its entire length.

There were usually two or three lines of trenches, joined by communications trenches that ran back to safer areas. Between the trenches and the enemy were belts of barbed wire to stop attackers from sneaking up.

A Day in a Soldier's Life

Having cold, wet feet for days on end caused a serious problem called trench foot.

"Your feet swell up and go completely dead. You could stick a bayonet into them and not feel a thing..." When "the swelling begins to go down, it is then that the agony begins. I have heard men...scream with the pain and many have had to have their feet and legs amputated."

-Sergeant Harry Roberts, Royal Army Medical Corps

Soldiers usually spent a few days at a time in a front line trench before being rotated into a reserve position, then rest. In a typical year, a soldier might spend 70 days in the front line, 30 in support, 120 in reserve and 70 at rest. If he were lucky, he would get about two weeks leave at home in that year.

A day began with stand-to in case of a dawn attack. Rifles were then cleaned and inspected and breakfast served. The day was spent in filling sandbags, repairing the trench and general chores. Men had free time during the day, but not much to do in it except to try and snatch a little sleep. At dusk, the stand-to was repeated, then the real work began. Darkness was the only time work could be done above ground. Wire had to be repaired, new trenches dug, supplies brought up and raids on the enemy carried out. Perhaps a couple of hours sleep, and the day's round began again with stand-to.

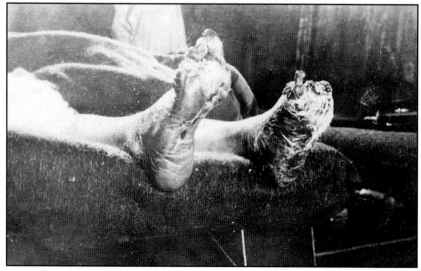

A case of trench foot

Boredom

Life in the trenches was disgusting. The two major irritants were rats and lice. The rats sometimes grew as large as cats, but they were usually easy to see and could be hunted. The lice were a different story.

Every soldier in World War I had lice. Adult body lice are about the size of a sesame seed and live and lay their eggs in the seams of clothing. Their bites draw blood and itch. When out of the line, soldiers could bathe and have their clothing fumigated, but in the trenches they had to be more inventive.

A common pastime was for a group of soldiers to sit around a candle. As they talked, they would go through their shirts, collecting lice and dropping them onto a tobacco tin lid held over the candle flame. The lice would pop on the hot tin. This never got rid of all the lice, but it made the men feel they were doing something. The East London slang term for a louse was a chat, so the soldiers called this activity chatting. Think about that next time you are having a "chat" with someone.

Most of the time, the soldiers of the First World War were not fighting battles. Even in the front line trenches, life could be relatively peaceful, and many enemies facing each other across no man's land were content to live and let live.

When not on the front line, soldiers were either in reserve or support. This was not rest, as they were kept busy repairing roads, digging support trenches or carrying supplies forward. Even here, they were not safe. Long range German guns could fire shells far into the rear area and kill men a long way from the front line.

What spare time the soldiers had was spent having baths to try to get rid of the lice that crawled in their thousands over everyone, writing letters home or repairing and cleaning their equipment.

Canadians playing a game of cards in a shell hole, 1917

Sometimes soccer matches against rival companies or battalions were arranged, and evenings were spent in estaminets.

Estaminets were small cafés, often set up in the parlour of a local house. Soldiers would cram in and sit at whatever tables had been scrounged from damaged houses nearby and talk or play cards. They were usually served cheap red or white wine by the madam, whose husband and sons were, most likely, in the French Army.

Nurses

It was almost as difficult being a doctor or nurse during the war as it was being a soldier. These people also faced dangers and had the daunting task of trying to heal horrible wounds and comfort soldiers in pain. Many brave women and men in the medical service risked their lives during the war.

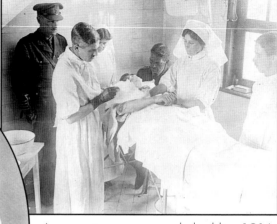

An operation on a wounded soldier, 1916

A Nursing Sister. Nursing Sisters was the title given to nurses in the Canadian military.

In the 1917 general election, Nursing Sisters and women who had relatives in the military were allowed to vote. Other Canadian women were not granted this right until the following year.

The funeral of a Nursing Sister killed during a German air raid, 1918

Prime Minister Borden visiting a Canadian hospital during the war

The Soft Underbelly

The year 1916 was a major disappointment for the Allies. It was to have been the year they won the war. Simultaneous attacks on all fronts, by Britain, France, Russia and Italy were supposed finally to defeat Germany and Austria. Unfortunately, the plans were disrupted by the German attack at Verdun and the Austrian attack at Trentino in Italy in May. The British attack on the Somme failed, and the Russian attack, despite Brusilov's success, did not end the war. By the end of 1916, everyone was resigned to a long war where the winner would be the side which could last the longest. There was still hope of victory on all sides, but no one anticipated the dramatic events that would shake the world and completely alter the face of the war in 1917.

Despite the disaster at Gallipoli in 1915, the idea that a campaign fought somewhere other than the trenches of France could produce a victory, without such vast casualties as the Somme, still persisted.

Even while Gallipoli was still being fought over, a British army was fighting its way along the Tigris River toward Baghdad, in what is now Iraq. They didn't get there, being defeated forty miles short of the city. The army retreated to the town of Kut, where they were besieged for 148 days before surrendering in April 1916. It was the largest surrender of British soldiers since Yorktown during the American War of Independence.

Also in late 1915, British and French troops landed at Salonika in Greece to try to help Serbia. Although Greece was a neutral country at the time, and they failed to prevent Serbia's defeat, the British and French stayed until the end of the war, when they finally managed to march north.

Indian soldiers fighting in Iraq. India (including today's Pakistan and Bangladesh) was ruled by the British at that time.

One of ironies of the First World War was that the very existence of an almost impregnable trench system in France meant that it was there that most of the fighting had to occur.

The search for an "easy" way to end the war without having to slog through Ypres or the Somme was an illusion. Whoever won would need to defeat the strongest forces the opposition had—if they were on the Western Front, that was where victory would have to occur. If one side moved their main strength elsewhere, then either the other side would break through in France or also move their main strength to the same place, thus creating the trenches in a new location. The result was a permanent deadlock.

More soldiers died in Salonika from malaria than from enemy action.

The most successful attack of the whole war took place in 1916 in Russia. Throughout June, July and August, the armies of Russian General Aleksei Brusilov captured 15,000 square miles of territory, took 450,000 prisoners, forced Austria to abandon an attack on Italy and compelled Germany to halt its attack on Verdun. They almost knocked the Austro-Hungarian Empire out of the war completely. Brusilov ultimately failed because his attacks were not supported by other Russian armies, and he ran out of reserves and ammunition.

By the end of 1916, most of Europe and beyond was involved in war.

General Brusilov

Future Canadian prime minister Lester B. Pearson served at Salonika, Greece in the Canadian Army Medical Corps. This picture was taken in 1916. He won the Nobel Peace Prize in 1957 and was elected prime minister in 1963.

Total War

The British navy blockaded Germany, preventing supplies reaching it, so the Germans tried to do the same to Britain using a new weapon, the submarine. At various times, Germany launched campaigns of unrestricted submarine warfare, which meant that any ship carrying supplies to Britain could be sunk without warning.

When the RMS *Lusitania* was torpedoed off the coast of Ireland, the British newspapers screamed about how barbaric it was to sink a passenger liner. It was only after the war that it was discovered that the *Lusitania* was carrying ammunition for Britain. It was probably also loaded with explosives, which blew up after the torpedo struck and caused the ship to sink in only eighteen minutes. It was illegal to carry explosives on passenger ships, so they were not listed among the vessel's cargo, but a very large amount of cheese was put on the list. However, the *Lusitania* had no refrigeration, and so could not carry cheese across the Atlantic.

The presence of explosives and ammunition made the *Lusitania* a legitimate war target for the submarine, but no one said that at the time.

In 1917, the First World War became a total war. No one expected quick victory any longer, so the resources of entire nations became dedicated to slogging it out until one side broke. Russia collapsed into revolution and the French army into mutiny. By the end of the year, Britain was the only one of the Allies capable of launching a major offensive, but there was a new player on the horizon.

While millions died in Europe, a war of words was going on across the Atlantic. Most Americans did not want to become involved in a European war. They were happy to stay neutral and sell food and material to the combatants, mostly Britain and France. However, some Americans wanted to take sides. There was considerable pressure from Americans of German descent to support their former country. Unfortunately for them, Germany was losing the propaganda war.

The *Lusitania*

YOU DRIVE A CAR HERE
—WHY NOT A TRANSPORT
IN FRANCE?

AMERICAN
FIELD SERVICE

Britain worked hard to present Germany as the aggressor in the war, and the papers were full of stories of German atrocities, some true, some fictional. America came close to declaring war on Germany in 1915 when a submarine torpedoed the liner *Lusitania,* and 128 American passengers drowned.

The last straw for the Americans came in February 1917 when a telegram from Germany to Mexico was intercepted and decoded by the British. The telegram suggested that Mexico and Germany form an alliance against America. A surge of anti-German feeling swept across the United States and, on April 6, the United States declared war on Germany.

It would be a long time before enough American soldiers could be trained and sent to Europe to make a difference, but the United States' vast resources doomed Germany in the long run.

When the United States entered the war, its government also produced enlistment posters.

Disrupted Plans

General Nivelle

The British and French had plans for a major joint offensive in 1917 but, just as Verdun had upset their plans in 1916, the Germans surprised them again. This time the surprise was not a major attack, but a withdrawal to immensely strong fortified positions, the Hindenburg Line.

The Hindenburg Line shortened the German trench system, freeing troops for the reserves. It also meant that any Allied attack had to cross a wasteland, more than sixty kilometres wide in some places, of destroyed villages, barren countryside and poisoned wells. But there was one Allied general who thought he had the answer.

General Robert Nivelle had become commander of the French Armies in late 1916. He promised to blast a hole through the German lines in only forty-eight hours in what became known as the Nivelle Offensive. Many people were against Nivelle's plan, and the Germans knew it was coming, but it went ahead on April 16 anyway. It was the same old story of unbroken wire, artillery and machine guns. The French Army suffered almost 200,000 casualties in two weeks. It was not a greater tragedy than the many others of the war, but Nivelle had promised quick victory and failed. He was fired.

The French mutinies were not entirely due to Nivelle's blunder. Conditions for French soldiers were much worse than for either the British or Germans. Pay, food and leave were poor and uncertain, and discipline was harsh. Relieving British troops often complained about the sorry state of French trenches. On top of it all, because of the way units were rotated into the front lines, almost the entire French Army had suffered through the horrors of Verdun.

The first mutiny was typical. On April 29th, 1917, the 2nd battalion of the 18th Infantry Regiment was ordered back to the front lines. They had suffered 600 casualties a few days before and had been promised rest. Having drunk a lot of wine, the soldiers became brave enough to refuse and began shouting "Down with the war."

As the men sobered up, the officers managed to persuade them to return to the front, but about a dozen soldiers were arrested, and five were sentenced to be shot.

The French generals feared revolution, but it didn't happen—at least not in France.

For the French Army, Nivelle's failure was too much. Throughout the spring of 1917, fifty-four divisions mutinied. Thousands of soldiers refused to obey their officers or deserted. One regiment went to the front bleating like sheep being led to the slaughter. Incredibly, the French managed to keep the mutinies secret, and the Germans were never able to take advantage of the chaos.

In the aftermath, 23,000 French soldiers were found guilty, and 432 sentenced to death. Only 55 were officially shot, but many other deaths were probably recorded as battle casualties. The French Army was wrecked. It would defend, but a major offensive was now beyond it. That would have to be up to the British.

A 1917 mutineer faces a firing squad.

Canadian Victory

Artillery fire killed and wounded more men than anything else in the war. But if used properly, it could save lives by ensuring that the slaughter of the first day of the Somme was not repeated. It was Canadians who perfected the use of artillery before Vimy.

Spotting where hidden enemy guns were was vital in protecting attacking troops. Since camouflaged guns were difficult to find, they had to be found by spotting the muzzle flashes or finding where the sound came from. The Canadian spotters allowed their artillery to destroy 86% of the German guns.

Another Canadian innovation was the use of machine guns in support of the artillery. The hail of bullets from these rapid-firing guns prevented the Germans from making repairs in trenches and bringing up supplies. The Germans called the days before Vimy "The Week of Suffering".

Canadian machine gunners, 1916

To support Nivelle, the British agreed to launch attacks around Arras. These were timed to begin before Nivelle attacked, so that the Germans would commit their reserves.

A crucial attack would be on Vimy Ridge, a seven-kilometre long hill that dominated the Allied positions. The task of taking this formidable position was given to the four Canadian divisions, working together for the first time in the war. They would be attacking over a graveyard where 100,000 Frenchmen had become casualties in failed assaults in 1915 and 1916.

Sir Julian Byng, the Canadian commander, demanded rigorous preparations. Tunnels were dug so that troops could be brought up without the Germans seeing them; huge storerooms were built to house the supplies needed for such a vast endeavour; the soldiers were given specific roles (bombers, riflemen, machine gunners) and trained for weeks on landscape similar to the ridge. Most importantly, the Canadian artillery, packed behind the front at one gun every eight metres, developed new techniques for finding and destroying the German guns and supporting the attack.

Canadians at Vimy Ridge

Canadians in the rubble of the main street of Vimy

A view from the crest of Vimy Ridge showing the village

Shrapnel bursting over troops digging themselves in at Vimy Ridge

A memorial to the Canadian dead at Vimy, 1917

At five thirty on the morning of April 9, as icy sleet lashed the battlefield, more than fifteen thousand Canadians left their trenches. As the earth shook and brightly coloured flares screamed for help from the German trenches, men from Halifax to Vancouver stormed forward behind a moving curtain of exploding shells. As long as they stayed close to the frightful creeping barrage, they were safe. Stunned German soldiers surrendered to the heavily armed men leaping into their trenches. By afternoon, the Canadians were on the summit of the ridge.

Celebrating Canadian troops returning from Vimy Ridge

Despite all the planning, the task had not been easy. Canadian soldiers showed extraordinary bravery and initiative, storming machine guns and continuing to attack even after their officers had been killed. The highest point of the ridge, where the soaring Vimy Memorial stands today, was taken in a bayonet charge against machine guns. In all, 3,598 Canadians died and 7,000 were wounded before the fighting on the ridge died down on April 12.

Vimy Ridge was an extraordinary victory, and it was a Canadian victory. Many people believe that Canada came of age as a country on those shell-scarred slopes on April 9, 1917.

A Canadian Hero

Thain
Wendell
MacDowell

Thain Wendell MacDowell from Lachute, Quebec was a captain in the 38th Battalion and one of four Canadian Victoria Cross winners at Vimy Ridge.

With only two privates as companions, MacDowell found himself isolated in front of the German third line of defence. His unit was being slaughtered by intense fire, so MacDowell rushed two machine gun nests, killing the occupants of one and driving off the others.

One of the German gunners disappeared into a deep bunker. Following the man into the darkness, MacDowell stumbled into seventy-seven members of the elite Prussian Guard. Thinking quickly, he shouted back along the tunnel as if he had supporting troops nearby and demanded the Germans' surrender. They all raised their hands, but how could he send them back into the open, where they would soon see they had been tricked?

Keeping incredibly calm, MacDowell sent his prisoners up the steps in batches of twelve, where they were disarmed and sent to the rear by his two companions. Only one man tried to resist by reaching for his rifle. He was shot dead.

Incredibly, this was not the first time MacDowell had done this. During the battle of the Somme, he had won another medal for subduing three German machine guns and capturing fifty-three Germans.

Revolution

Nicholas became Czar of Russia on the death of his father, Alexander, in 1894. His reign began badly when more than a thousand people died in a crowd stampede during his coronation. Nicholas never managed to cope with the changing world of modern technology and ideas. He was a quiet man who valued his family but had trouble being an inspiring figurehead.

The situation was complicated by the fact that his son suffered from hemophilia, a disorder that prevented his blood from clotting, meaning that the slightest injury could kill him.

When war broke out in 1914, Nicholas took charge of the army but neglected domestic matters, and his country slid gradually into chaos, then revolution.

Czar Nicholas II

Defeat in war encourages revolution. In 1905, Russia was defeated by Japan, and revolution broke out across the country. It failed and was put down brutally everywhere, but it was a warning.

In 1917, Russia had not been defeated, but things were not going well. Huge areas of the country were occupied by the enemy, the army was poorly equipped and badly led, and a harsh winter and food shortages made life intolerable. In March, food riots broke out in Petrograd (now St. Petersburg), and soldiers refused to fire on the rioters. When Czar Nicholas II, the Russian monarch, attempted to return to his capital, he was prevented by soldiers and railway workers. The Russian generals advised the Czar to abdicate, and the monarchy in Russia came to an end.

Councils of workers and soldiers, "soviets", became very powerful, and a Provisional Government was set up. No one talked about stopping the war—the Czar was blamed for all the problems—and the other Allies welcomed the revolution. Russia would become a democracy.

Everyone was happy, except Vladimir Ilyich Ulyanov. He was the leader of a small revolutionary party that believed that all governments needed to be overthrown and that revolution had to spread throughout the world.

Lenin

Vladimir Ilyich Ulyanov was born in 1870, the son of a successful official. His older brother was hanged as a revolutionary in 1887. Lenin followed in his brother's footsteps to become a revolutionary agitator. He adopted the political philosophies of Karl Marx and gradually rose to prominence in the Russian revolutionary movement. Though there were other strong leaders in the Bolshevik faction of the Russian communists, such as Leon Trotsky and Joseph Stalin, Lenin was the unquestioned leader at the time of the 1917 uprising. After his death in 1924, Stalin seized the leadership of the Soviet Union in a power struggle and ruled the country until his death in 1953.

Like many revolutionaries, Ulyanov used a code name, Lenin. When the Czar abdicated, Lenin was desperate to lead a more extreme revolution than the Provisional Government wanted, but there was a problem. Lenin was living in exile in neutral Switzerland. To get home to Petrograd, Lenin would have to cross a war-torn continent.

The one country prepared to help Lenin return home was Russia's enemy, Germany. The Germans thought that Lenin would stir up trouble in Russia and weaken its resolve to fight. Their plan succeeded beyond their wildest dreams.

In secret, Lenin and some of his companions boarded a sealed train. As it crossed Germany, they were not allowed to leave their carriage. After a detour through Scandinavia, Lenin arrived in Petrograd on April 16. Courtesy of his country's enemies, Lenin was now in a position to take power and stamp his name on world history.

The Bolsheviks
Take Power

Communism is a form of socialism that promotes a society where there are no separate classes of people, and where everyone shares in ownership of the industry and resources. Its founder was Karl Marx who believed that a communist society would be fair and that everyone would have the same opportunities. Some famous Canadians, like Norman Bethune, were communists, but the system has never worked for long in practice when it has been tried on a national scale, as it was in Russia after the revolution of 1917.

Throughout the summer of 1917, Russia struggled on with the war. In July, the army launched a major offensive that collapsed after a few days. The soldiers could take no more. Revolutionary councils met, unpopular officers were shot, and tens of thousands of men simply went home. The army collapsed.

In Petrograd, Lenin's Bolshevik party was small but, in the midst of chaos, it was the only organized group. On November 6, the Bolsheviks seized the post office, the telegraph exchange and the railway stations. The following day, with the loss of six lives, they stormed the Winter Palace and arrested the members of the Provisional Government.

Lenin, now the virtual dictator of Russia, called for peace. On December 15, Russia and Germany signed an armistice. The war in the east was over, and the Allies had lost a major partner. Germany now had the single front war it had wanted since 1914, but could the Germans take advantage of the situation before the Americans arrived in overwhelming numbers?

Demonstrators in Petrograd

Spreading Revolution

The war had never been popular in Quebec, where many saw it as a European war with little to do with them. Conscription was hated in Quebec, but it was not popular in English-speaking Canada either. Of the more than 400,000 called up for military service under the Conscription Act, 380,510 appealed. Hundreds refused to go and went into hiding to avoid being called up.

One of them, a union activist named Albert "Ginger" Goodwin from the coal mines of Vancouver Island, hid with other men in the hills. The government hunted the men down, and on a hot July day in 1918, Goodwin was shot and killed. The circumstances were suspicious, and Goodwin became a hero to socialists and pacifists across Western Canada.

Lenin was not the only one calling for peace in 1917, and Russia wasn't the only country where revolution was possible. The French Army had mutinied, and German sailors did the same. Strikes by workers in Britain were increasing, and socialists spoke out against the war. President Wilson in America called for peace and published fourteen points that he hoped would lead to a just peace and no more war.

Even in Canada, there was unrest. By 1917, there were no more volunteers, and the Canadian army in France, despite its victory at Vimy, was being worn down.

Conscription, which meant that every fit man was liable to be called up and sent to fight, was introduced and made law after Prime Minister Borden won the election in December.

An anti-conscription parade in Montreal, 1917

Some Success

There were actually twenty-one mines beneath Messines Ridge, but two of them failed to explode, and their locations were lost after the war. One blew up in a thunderstorm on the 17th of June, 1955. It scared the local inhabitants and killed an unsuspecting cow. The location of the other unexploded mine is suspected, but no one wants to dig down to the extremely unstable explosives to be sure.

Vimy Ridge was not the only success of 1917. Two others bracketed the horrors of Passchendaele, which took place in July, 1917.

On June 7, a million pounds of explosives, packed by the British into nineteen deep mines under the German defences on Messines Ridge, near Ypres, were detonated by the Allies. The explosion could be heard in London, and the German defences and defenders disappeared. With minimal Allied casualties, the attackers took the entire ridge.

Messines was a dramatic success for the Allies, but one that was hard to repeat. The mines had taken two years to build and pack with explosives, and the troops advanced three kilometres. It would take a long time and cost many lives to get to Berlin, the German capital, at that rate.

The mud prevented the use of tanks at Passchendaele, but they were used soon after. Three hundred and eighty-one of them attacked over the dry ground in front of Cambrai on November 20. Their success was stunning. The tanks advanced five miles over a four mile front in just one day—farther than in all the bloody weeks of the Somme or Passchendaele, but no one knew what to do with the success. The attack petered out, and German counterattacks took back all the gains.

Vimy, Messines and Cambrai were not war-winning battles, but some generals were finally trying different tactics. Perhaps 1918 would be different.

Canadians of the 5th Canadian Mounted Regiment riding on a tank

Air War

On April 21, 1918, von Richthofen, the Red Baron, was chasing Canadian pilot Wilfred May. At the same time, he was being hunted by May's childhood friend Arthur "Roy" Brown. As Brown manoeuvred in for the kill, an Australian machine gunner on the ground hit von Richthofen's plane. The Red Baron managed to land his plane in a field in Allied territory but died moments later. The British buried him with full military honours.

Arthur Brown

While soldiers were drowning in mud around Ypres, an equally violent battle was raging in the skies above.

By 1917, the era of firing pistols at enemy aircraft was over. Multiple machine guns fired through the rotating propellors of fast, sturdy, manoeuverable killing machines. The aces of 1915 were innovative individualists who thought of themselves as Knights of the Air. Those of 1917 were systematic hunter-killers who sought their prey in packs.

Tactics had changed too. Aircraft were now specially designed for specific roles. Some were two-seaters that patrolled the enemy trenches and back areas, photographing and spotting for the artillery. These slow aircraft were protected by small, single-seater scouts whose job it was to fight off the enemy attackers—this is where the "aces" came in. Some scouts were used as ground attack aircraft, machine-gunning or bombing enemy trenches or bringing down observation balloons. Increasingly, as the war went on, multi-engined planes lumbered overhead to drop large bomb loads far to the rear of the front line.

But, despite the increasing organization of the air war, there was still room for individuality. The German aces, led by von Richthofen in his red triplane, often painted their machines in garish colours.

The pilot and observer of a balloon, 1916

58

Passchendaele

Apart from Vimy, other attacks around Arras bogged down in the usual high casualties, but General Haig, the British commander, wanted to try again. If the French couldn't help, he would do it alone. Against the advice of many of his staff, Haig planned a third major battle around the town of Ypres.

On July 31, the British attacked, not in neat rows as they had on the Somme—something had been learned in the past year. But the result was the same: tens of thousands of dead men for a few metres of ground. Third Ypres, or Passchendaele as it was known, named after the village that was one of the objectives, was different in another way and produced its own special horror.

The ground around Ypres was clay. Water didn't drain through it, so when it rained, the ground became a sea of mud. It rained heavily that summer and fall of 1917. In places, the mud reached men's chests. The wounded fell in and drowned, horses, guns and tanks sank from sight.

A wounded Canadian carried to an aid post through the mud and water at Passchendaele

The battlefield around the village of Passchendaele was turned into a sea of mud.

Passchendaele, Ypres and most other devastated towns were meticulously rebuilt after the war using old plans and photographs. However, some places simply ceased to exist.

Dousumont was a village of fifty houses about six kilometres from Verdun. In the spring of 1916, German artillery reduced the town to little more than dust. Now all that marks the site of this community are fifty squares marked out on the unbroken grass. Each square bears the name and occupation of a villager.

Sometimes it took a dozen men just to carry a wounded man back to solid ground.

This nightmare in the mud waxed and waned for almost four months, and over 300,000 British soldiers were killed or wounded. One story tells of a staff officer being taken, near the end of the battle, on his first tour of the front. When he saw the mud, he burst into tears and said "Good God, did we really send men to fight in that?" His companion simply replied, "It's worse further up."

The battle ended in early November, when Canadian troops finally took the patch of stained ground where Passchendaele village had once stood.

Scenes of Passchendaele: Canadian soldiers using shell holes for cover (left);
a soldier struggles through the mud and barbed wire (right).

Multicultural Canada in the War

African-Canadian soldiers in a captured German dug-out, 1918

Some Canadians were heroes just by getting into the army. When fifty Black Canadians attempted to volunteer in Nova Scotia, they were told, "This is not for you fellows, this is a white man's war." Many, including Black Americans who crossed the border to enlist, persevered, and some segregated units were eventually formed. The Number Two Construction Battalion was the first Black unit to serve in the war. They did not receive the same supplies as other battalions and did not receive treatment equal to other soldiers, but they were proud to serve.

Aboriginal Canadians were not allowed to enlist before 1915, but eventually 3,500 did. Japanese Canadians also had to struggle to sign up. Despite their enthusiasm and dedication, these groups were never fully accepted and always had to battle against the racism of their own side, as well as against the enemy.

Aboriginal volunteers pose before leaving for Europe

Billy Bishop

Raymond Collishaw survived the war, and a tour fighting in Russia in 1919, to become an Air Vice Marshall in World War II. There is a beautiful replica of his Sopwith Triplane in the Calgary Aerospace Museum and the airport in his home town on Vancouver Island was named Nanaimo-Collishaw Air Terminal in 1999 in his honour.

Billy Bishop, the top Canadian ace with seventy-two "kills", painted the nose of his plane bright blue, and Raymond Collishaw, only ten "kills" behind Bishop, led a squadron in his Black Sopwith Triplane, Black Maria.

Bishop was a controversial figure. He began as an observer but soon took his pilot exam, which he barely passed. His colourful career included a dogfight with the Red Baron and an incident that is still in dispute today.

One morning in 1917, Bishop took off alone and attacked a German aerodrome. In his report, Bishop claimed to have shot down three planes. No one could confirm it, but Bishop was awarded the Victoria Cross for bravery.

Billy Bishop in 1917

The Sopwith Triplane at the Calgary Aerospace Museum

Major Barker's Bravery

The Victoria Cross was introduced in 1856 for "...most conspicuous bravery, or some daring or preeminent act of valour or self-sacrifice, or extreme devotion to duty in the presence of the enemy." 1356 have been awarded since then, ninety-four to Canadians or Newfoundlanders, seventy-two of which were during the First World War. In 1993, a Canadian Victoria Cross was established, but it has yet to be won.

On patrol the morning of October 27, 1918, the last day before he returned to his training duties in England, Canadian Major William Barker attacked a German two-seater, which he destroyed. Despite being wounded in the thigh, Barker then shot down another plane. Attacked from all sides, he was severely wounded but still managed to fight on. He passed out, recovered and shot down yet another before a bullet shattered his left elbow.

Slipping in and of consciousness, Barker continued to fight, taking down another enemy plane before managing to fight his way back to his lines and crash landing. For fighting against over sixty enemy aircraft and shooting down four, Barker was also rewarded with the Victoria Cross.

Major William Barker

Barker in a Sopwith Camel fighter plane

Poets

The poetry of Wilfred Owen, along with books like *All Quiet on the Western Front* by Erich Maria Remarque, did much to show people who had not experienced the war what it was really like. Even today, almost a hundred years later, the poems of Wilfred Owen, Siegfried Sassoon and Isaac Rosenberg still have the power to shock us.

Wilfred Owen was killed by machine gun fire a week before the war ended. He was twenty-five years old.

As the soldiers and generals struggled to come to terms with the new warfare, writers tried equally hard to express the experience. The most successful were the soldier-poets who created a whole new type of poetry.

In 1914, a poet going to war, Julian Grenfell, could write:

> *And life is colour and warmth and light,*
> *And a striving evermore for these;*
> *And he is dead who will not fight;*
> *And who dies fighting has increase.*

He is talking about how wonderful the world is and how noble it is to go to war and perhaps die.

By 1917, another poet who has seen the horrors of war, Wilfred Owen, describes soldiers:

> *Bent double, like old beggars under sacks,*
> *Knock-kneed, coughing like hags, we cursed through sludge...*
> *Men marched asleep. Many had lost their boots*
> *But limped on, blood-shod. All went lame; all blind...*

The romance of war has vanished. Sick, exhausted soldiers simply struggled on.

Wilfred Owen

In Flanders Fields

One of the most famous poems of the First World War was written by a Canadian doctor, John McCrae, after his friend had been killed.

In Flanders Fields

In Flanders fields the poppies blow
Between the crosses, row on row,
*   That mark our place; and in the sky*
*   The larks, still bravely singing, fly*
Scarce heard amid the guns below.

We are the Dead. Short days ago
We lived, felt dawn, saw sunset glow,
*   Loved and were loved, and now we lie*
*   In Flanders fields.*

Take up our quarrel with the foe:
To you from failing hands we throw
*   The torch; be yours to hold it high.*
*   If ye break faith with us who die*
We shall not sleep, though poppies grow
*   In Flanders fields.*

In 1914, John McCrae shares a lighter moment with his dog

John Alexander McCrae (1872 to 1918) was born in Guelph, Ontario, and studied medicine at the University of Toronto. He served in the Boer War and was a surgeon with the Canadian Artillery in 1915 when his friend Lieutenant Alexis Helmer was killed. "In Flanders Fields" was printed in the English magazine *Punch* and became immediately popular. McCrae regarded his fame with amusement and went on to command the No.3 Canadian General Hospital at Boulogne, France. He died there of pneumonia on January 28th, 1918.

The Last Gamble

By the beginning of 1918, the Germans knew the war was lost unless they could win it before the Americans arrived in force. In a last, desperate gamble, they hurled the units freed from the Russian campaign into a series of devastating attacks against the British and French.

New tactics—small groups of heavily armed, highly trained storm troops dashing forward behind creeping barrages—worked well initially, and the Allies were thrown back in panic and confusion, but the old rules still applied. A defender could always move his reserves to a threatened area faster than an attacker's soldiers could walk across a devastated battlefield. The German attacks were halted.

In five major offensives between March 21 and late July, the Germans captured thousands of prisoners, piles of equipment and many times the territory that the Allies had taken in France or Belgium in four years. They had swept forward in a way not seen since 1914 and were within artillery range of Paris, but they were exhausted and beaten. Now it was the Allies' turn.

On April 11, when the German offensive was at its height and things looked blackest for the Allies, General Haig issued his famous "backs to the wall" Order of the Day.

"Words fail me to express the admiration which I feel for the splendid resistance offered by all ranks of our Army under the most trying circumstances…

"There is no other course open to us but to fight it out. Every position must be held to the last man: there must be no retirement. With our backs to the wall and believing in the justice of our cause each one of us must fight on to the end. The safety of our homes and the Freedom of mankind alike depend upon the conduct of each one of us at this critical moment." Of course, Haig was being far too dramatic, but it shows the general feeling of desperation after so many dark years of war.

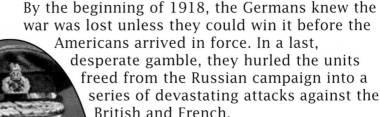

General Haig

Americans at Last

Despite the passion that recent immigrants to America felt about the war in Europe, many could not see why their country should become involved in what they saw as the Old World's squabbles. The President, Woodrow Wilson, thought America should become involved so that they could solve all the problems in Europe that had led to the war. However, he could not have persuaded enough people without the intercepted German telegram suggesting an alliance with Mexico. Even after America declared war on Germany, there were doubts. Britain and France wanted Wilson to send over as many soldiers as soon as possible to shore up their suffering armies. The American generals didn't want their soldiers to be sucked into the horrors of the previous years and insisted on waiting until an American army under American officers was ready to fight.

Even as the Germans were pushing the Allies back in the spring of 1918, the Americans were preparing to make their contribution to the war. On May 28, the American 1st Division took the village of Cantigny. It was a small action, but it was the first time the Americans were in battle on their own.

On June 3/4, the Americans attacked again at Château-Thierry and pushed the Germans back. Encouraged by these small successes, General Pershing ordered the marines of the American 2nd Division to capture Belleau Wood.

On the morning of June 6, the marines attacked across open cornfields in the face of heavy machine gun fire. They learned what the British had learned on the Somme and suffered heavily. They gained a foothold in the wood, but it was not until June 26, after they had attacked another five times and beaten off numerous German counterattacks, that the wood was secure.

The Americans suffered almost 10,000 dead and wounded at Belleau Wood. It wasn't on the scale of Passchendaele, but the new ally had served notice that it was going to be a factor in the war.

American soldiers in action at Belleau Wood

The End of Monarchy in Russia

One reason for the unpopularity of the Czar and his family was a mystic called Grigori Rasputin. Rasputin gained influence with the royal family, especially the Empress Alexandra, by helping their son Alexei through an illness. However, after the war broke out, he began to argue for a Russian withdrawal from the fighting. On December 16th, 1916, Rasputin was assassinated by a group of Russian nobles. What exactly happened that night has always been in doubt and various stories have claimed that Rasputin died from poison, shooting, beating or drowning. Recent evidence has come to light suggesting that a British spy, worried that Russia might sign a separate peace treaty with Germany, may have fired the fatal shot.

After he abdicated, the Czar and his family were held prisoner by Lenin's government. As civil war raged across Russia, they were moved around and ended up in a house in Yekaterinburg near the Ural Mountains.

In the early hours of July 17, 1918, the Czar, his wife, three daughters, son and family servants were woken up and hustled down to a basement room. There a local official read a death sentence and, as the Czar screamed, "Lord, oh my God! Oh my God! What is this?" soldiers opened fire.

All were killed, although some of the children may have survived for some time as the bullets bounced off the jewels the girls had hidden in their corsets. Attempts were made to burn the bodies, after which they were buried in a remote spot.

For years, rumours persisted that at least one of the daughters, Anastasia, had miraculously survived, and several people came forward to say they were the princess. However, a group of skeletons was discovered in the woods near Yekaterinburg in 1991, and DNA tests proved that they were the Czar and his entire family.

The Devil's Chariots

The first tank versus tank battle in history occurred on April 24, 1918. Lieutenant F. Mitchell was in command of the British tank. Three of his crew of seven had been gassed before he spotted an A7V.

"There, some 300 yards away, a round, squat-looking monster was advancing. Behind it came waves of infantry, and further away to left and right crawled two more of these armed tortoises...

"Suddenly, against our steel wall, a hurricane of hail pattered, and the interior was filled with myriads of sparks and flying splinters. Something rattled against the steel helmet of the driver sitting next to me, and my face was stung with minute fragments of steel...

"I took a risk and stopped the tank for a moment.

"The pause was justified; a carefully aimed shot hit the turret of the German tank, bringing it to a standstill." Mitchell's gunner hit the German tank twice more, knocking it onto its side. Little did he know he had won an historic engagement that would be repeated thousands of times in wars to come.

An A7V tank

One invention that had a limited effect in this war but which went on to become a decisive weapon in the Second World War was the tank. Invented in Britain in 1915 as a way to crush barbed wire and cross enemy trenches, tanks were so named to conceal their real nature from spies. Workers in the factories that built them were told they were working on mobile water tanks.

Tanks were either armed with machine guns or two six-pounder cannons and had armour that could stop bullets. A few were used at the Somme, Arras and Passchendaele, but they were slow, prone to breakdowns and getting stuck in the mud. When enough of them were concentrated on dry ground, they could have a dramatic impact, but they never had the range to exploit a breakthrough.

Between them, France and Britain produced over 6,000 tanks. The Germans mainly used captured tanks but did make one of their own, the huge A7V. It was very heavy, and only twenty were ever made.

Life inside the early tanks was brutal. It was dark, hot, uncomfortable, noisy and smelled strongly of gasoline. When under fire, chips from the armour flew around, and tanks had a tendency to burst into flames.

All in all, tanks in World War I had limited use, but their potential led to the armoured divisions that roared across France and Russia a generation later.

Amiens and the Last Hundred Days

The Battle of Amiens was important not only for the ground, prisoners and guns taken, but for a radical change in perspective. After years of being stuck in trenches with little chance of breaking out, battles were now being fought in open country. Suddenly it seemed as if the war might end after all. The Allied armies were keen to press on and end the war, while the Germans were desperately trying to hold out. The only German hope left after Amiens was not for victory but for a negotiated peace.

With the German offensive exhausted, the Allies fought back, and it was the Canadians who led the way. Much less well known than Vimy Ridge, but probably more important in terms of winning the war, was the Canadian attack outside Amiens on August 8.

At 4:20 in the morning, in thick fog, without a long barrage to warn the enemy and supported by hundreds of tanks, the 1st, 2nd and 3rd Canadian Divisions crashed through the German defences southwest of Amiens. By 7:30, they had gained their objectives, and the 4th Division passed through to continue the attack.

That day, the Canadians advanced eleven kilometres into open country, took thousands of prisoners and hundreds of guns. Over the following hundred days, the Canadians continued to be at the forefront of the advance, and on November 10, the last full day of fighting, liberated the town of Mons, where the British war had begun fifty months and millions of casualties before.

There were bigger advances in the last hundred days of the First World War than on August 8, but that was the day that Ludendorff, the German commander, called "the black day of the German Army." The Battle of Amiens destroyed the morale of the German soldiers and buoyed the Allies. After August 8, there was no doubt who would eventually win.

German prisoners captured by Canadians at Amiens

The Last Shots

Few front-line soldiers celebrated wildly on November 11th, 1918. They were too numbed by what they had been through, and too many friends had died for them to celebrate. It was different among civilians. Wild street parties broke out spontaneously in cities all over the world. As the church bells tolled for only the second time in four years, people streamed onto streets across the British Empire and began partying. Canadian and Australian soldiers had a food fight with Brussels sprouts in London, and a fire the Canadians started at the base of Nelson's column in Trafalgar Square left scars that can still be seen today.

There was a prophecy among the troops in France in 1918 that the end of the war would be signalled by four invisible black flares being fired into the night sky, so that no one would know, and the fighting would go on forever. In fact, it was signalled by eerie silence.

During the foggy night of November 6/7, spurred on by mutiny and revolution behind them in Germany, a German delegation crossed the French lines in a series of cars draped in white flags. In a railway carriage in woods outside Paris, they were handed the harsh Allied terms for an Armistice. Three days later, the Armistice was signed and, at 11 a.m. on Monday, November 11, 1918, the guns at last fell silent.

In many places, the fighting died down as news spread and 11 a.m. approached, but not everywhere. On the American front, the 313th Infantry Battalion charged some machine gun nests. Private Henry Guenther of Company A was shot to death. Almost as he hit the ground, the guns fell silent.

During November 10 and 11, the Canadian 2nd and 3rd Division suffered 481 men killed attacking Mons. At 9:30, a British officer attached to the Canadian Corps was killed. He had fought at Mons in August 1914.

Canadians march through Mons on the morning of November 11, 1918

Influenza

People die in Canada every winter from the flu. Usually, they are those with least resistance, the very young and the very old. In 1918/19, one in six Canadians caught the flu, and it cruelly did the most damage among the young and healthy, those between twenty and forty years old.

The health services were overwhelmed by the scale of the disaster. The streets were deserted, people wore masks, and streetcars were sprayed with disinfectant. People avoided each other, gatherings of six or more were banned and, in some places, shaking hands was a criminal offence. Some people burned incense or sulphur in their houses to try and ward off the virus. It was little use. Fifty thousand Canadians died in the influenza pandemic.

As the war swept toward its brutal conclusion in the fall of 1918, few were aware that nature had a cruel trick up its sleeve. It was a trick that would kill more people than the entire four years of war before it.

In the spring of 1918, influenza raced around the world. Millions suffered from three days of headaches, aching joints and high fever, and felt lethargic for about two weeks after. Most people recovered, although so many soldiers caught the flu that some attacks had to be postponed.

Then the flu went away, but while it was gone it was changing, mutating into something entirely different, something almost unimaginably hideous, which in a year would be the most deadly plague in human history.

Albertan men wearing masks during the flu pandemic

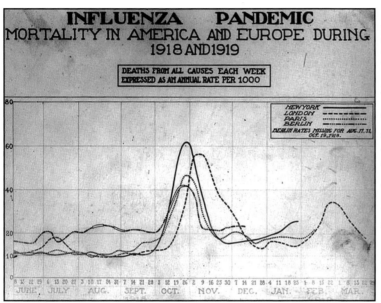

INFLUENZA PANDEMIC
MORTALITY IN AMERICA AND EUROPE DURING 1918 AND 1919

DEATHS FROM ALL CAUSES EACH WEEK
EXPRESSED AS AN ANNUAL RATE PER 1000

NEWYORK
LONDON
PARIS
BERLIN
BERLIN RATES MISSING FOR AUG. 17, 31, OCT. 19, 1918.

JUNE   JULY   AUG.   SEPT.   OCT.   NOV.   DEC.   JAN.   FEB.   MAR.

This graph shows the incredible, tragic effect of the flu on the death rate in 1919.

The plague returned in September. It began with a mild headache and burning eyes. Then the sufferer would begin to shiver, and no number of blankets could keep him or her warm. As patients drifted in and out of consciousness, their faces turned dark brown, and they began to cough up blood. In a terrifying matter of hours or, at most, a few days, lungs filled up and the victims drowned.

The flu didn't kill everyone. About 2.5% of people who caught it died, but that was enough. No continent or country escaped. Somewhere between 20 and 100 million people died. In the United States, the influenza epidemic killed more people than died in battle in the First and Second World Wars, Korean War and Vietnam combined.

Precautions did little good. The average American life expectancy dropped from around fifty-one years in 1917 to thirty-nine years in 1918. A tiny virus turned out to be a more efficient dealer of death than all the rifles, machine guns, bombs and artillery of a world war.

Peace Treaty

Some historians have suggested that it is not accurate to give the First and Second World Wars their own names. They argue that it was all one war, lasting from 1914-1945, with a twenty year truce in the middle.

Perhaps they are right, since the events of 1918 and 1919 did lead directly to World War II. It is all a matter of interpretation.

Once the shooting was over, the arguing began. After such a vast war that had brought revolutions, the abdications of kings and the collapse of empires, almost the entire world needed to be remade. But how?

Everyone at the Versailles Peace Conference, held outside of Paris in 1919, wanted something different. President Wilson of the United States wanted everyone to be able to determine their own futures, and for a world body to prevent anything like the war happening again.

Unfortunately, he didn't understand the complexities of European politics, and even his own Congress refused to support him at home.

Georges Clemenceau of France wanted to crush Germany so that it would never be a threat again. Unfortunately, the punitive payments that Germany was forced to pay crippled its economy and led to the massive dissatisfaction that helped Hitler to gain power a decade later.

World leaders at Versailles (left to right): Prime Ministers Vittorio Orlando (Italy), David Lloyd George (Britain), Georges Clemenceau (France) and President Woodrow Wilson (United States)

74

Three Allied leaders dominated the Peace conference. Unfortunately, they all had very different visions of what should be achieved. Woodrow Wilson, of the United States, wanted all European people to determine their own future and all future arguments to be decided by a League of Nations (an early version of today's United Nations). David Lloyd George, of Britain, wanted no one power to be dominant in Europe. Georges Clemenceau wanted to punish Germany for the war. On top of this, everyone else, from Italy and Romania to the Jews and Arabs in the Middle East, all had impossibly contradictory desires. The politicians who tried to remake the world at Versailles faced the same sorts of problems that the generals had in the war—finding simple solutions to complex problems and dealing with forces that they could only barely understand.

The conference table at Versailles

David Lloyd George of Britain wanted Germany's overseas empire. He got it, but the artificial borders that were drawn on maps, particularly in the Middle East where the Turkish empire had collapsed, held the seeds of conflicts that are still ongoing today.

Everybody else wanted something, and often the demands were contradictory. Whole new countries—Poland, Czechoslovakia, Austria, Hungary, Yugoslavia—were created from the ruins of Europe. Tens of thousands of square kilometres from the defeated powers were given to other nations. Millions of people suddenly found themselves citizens of different countries. Not all of them were happy, and that unhappiness frequently spilled over into bloodshed as the century wore on.

The Treaty of Versailles was a noble effort to make a better world. It failed because too many people wanted too many different things, and not everyone could be satisfied. Winston Churchill called Versailles "a sad case of complicated idiocy."

Europe 1919

Norway

Sweden

Finland

Denmark

Estonia

Latvia

Lithuania

East Prussia

Russia

United Kingdom

Netherlands

Germany

Poland

Belgium

Luxembourg

Czechoslovakia

France

Austria

Hungary

Switzerland

Romania

Italy

Yugoslavia

Spain

Bulgaria

Albania

Greece

Turkey

800 kilometres

This map shows the new political divisions of Europe decided on during the negotiations of the Treaty of Versailles. These borders remained until World War II.

The Cost

In the First World War, 616,557 men served in the Canadian armed forces, either at home or overseas. This was almost a third of the male population between ages eighteen and forty-five. Of these men, 155,799 were wounded and 60,383 died. Over 11,000 of them have no known grave and are commemorated at the huge Canadian memorial on the summit of Vimy Ridge.

A view of the devastation in Halifax, Nova Scotia, after the explosion in 1917

The casualties were not limited to France. On December 6, 1917, the munitions ship *Mont-Blanc* exploded in Halifax harbour in the greatest man-made explosion before nuclear weapons. Two thousand people died, six thousand more were seriously injured, and 2.5 square kilometres of the city were levelled. It brought war's suffering home to Canada.

Everyone in Canada was affected in one way or another by the First World War. Most people knew someone who had served or was wounded or killed. Canada didn't get any territory or empire at the peace conference, but the country got something more valuable.

Canada came out of the war much more of a nation than it had been before. The sacrifices of the Somme and Passchendaele and the victories of Vimy and Amiens had given many Canadians a common cause and a shared sense of sacrifice. Like Australia and New Zealand, by 1919, Canada was not just another dominion of Britain, it was a country in its own right.

Remembering

There are war memorials commemorating the First World War all around the world. In Sydney, Auckland, Toronto, London and countless towns and villages, sad lists of names are carved around the bases of bronze statues of soldiers or simple crosses. The dead from other wars have been added later, but they are always much shorter lists.

A bronze sculpture on the National War Memorial in Ottawa

The greatest concentration of memorials is in France and Belgium, and it defines the 700 kilometres of front lines where most soldiers died. In Ypres, there is the Menin gate, where the last post is still played every day at sunset. On the Somme, there is the Thiepval Memorial with 73,000 carved names of missing soldiers who died on the Somme. At Verdun there is a vast ossuary containing the bones of 130,000 unknown French and German soldiers. Between these sometimes ponderous masses of stone, there are hundreds of cemeteries, ranging from a few dozen graves to the almost 12,000 at Tyne Cot near Ypres.

It is a mind-numbing experience to go among them, but there is no better way to understand the magnitude and the cost of the First World War. It is a sobering experience to walk along a row of gravestones and suddenly realize that the oldest person there was only twenty-two years old and that the entire row died on the same day.

The frenzy to build memorials to the war dead indicates how shocking an experience it was and how fervently people hoped it wouldn't happen again. That hope was in vain. The Second World War was much worse, and wars are still fought today. Perhaps, one day, all the memorials won't be necessary to remind us of the horrible cost of war.

The Canadian National Vimy Memorial

After the horrors of trench warfare and unimaginable sacrifice during the battles of World War I, the Government of Canada initiated plans in 1921 for a national battlefield monument to be situated on Hill 145 at Vimy. In 1922, the French government ceded Vimy Ridge to Canada in perpetuity.

Toronto sculptor Walter Seymour Allward was the chosen designer after a competition consisting of 160 designs. He stated in a 1921 interview that his idea was inspired by a wartime dream that he had never forgotten. He dreamed he was in a great battlefield and saw Canadian troops going in by the thousands and being killed; then he saw thousands marching to their aid. "They were the dead. They rose in masses, filed silently by and entered the fight to aid the living. I have tried to show this in this monument to Canada's fallen, what we owed them and we will forever owe them." The monument was dedicated by King Edward on July 26, 1936. Inscribed on the memorial are the 11,285 names of those with no known grave.

Walter S. Allward (1875–1955) is buried in the churchyard of St. John's York Mills Anglican Church in Toronto. A historical plaque was dedicated in 2007 at his gravesite to honour his work in the commemoration of the loss of more than 60,000 Canadians in the war.

The restored monument was re-dedicated on Monday, April 9th, 2007 (the 90th anniversary of the Battle of Vimy Ridge) by Queen Elizabeth II.

The monument at Vimy Ridge took eleven years to build and used six thousand tons of limestone. Each of the twenty huge sculptures was carved in place and represents ideas like truth, knowledge and justice. The most poignant is the figure of a weeping woman, mourning the fallen Canadians.

Written by Jan Allward, a member of the Allward family, who attended the rededication ceremony at Vimy Ridge with other members of the Allward family in 2007.

Remember
Victory and Tragedy

There are two major Canadian memorials in France, one on the site of a victory, the other on the site of a tragedy.

The two white pillars of the memorial on Vimy Ridge can be seen for miles. At the base of the hill, reconstructed trenches and the underground tunnels where the soldiers waited to attack can be seen. Sheep graze among the trees, oblivious to the grassed-over shell craters.

The Newfoundland Memorial Park preserves the stretch of the front lines where the Newfoundland Regiment suffered horribly in July 1, 1916. The trenches are not reconstructed as at Vimy. Their sides have slumped, softening their edges, but they are no less moving because of that. It is possible to walk across the grass of no man's land from the Newfoundland trenches to the German ones, a pleasant stroll on a sunny afternoon today, but a horror for the young men who walked into the machine guns all those years ago.

It is important to remember our history, through visiting memorials or attending the ceremonies on November 11. The young men and boys who marched off to war so enthusiastically in the fall of 1914 came from a different world than ours, but they had the same hopes and fears as we do. Perhaps we have to understand them in order that future generations do not go marching off to other wars.

The tortured battlefields of the First World War are mostly pleasant, peaceful fields today, but death is lurking just beneath the surface. In 1991, thirty-six French farmers died when their farm machinery unearthed live ammunition as they ploughed their land. In 1998, 15,000 people near Vimy Ridge had to be evacuated while a large underground stockpile of bombs and shells was removed. Every spring, the roadsides of Flanders and the Somme are littered with piles of rusting shells awaiting bomb disposal experts to destroy them.

Millions of shells were fired between 1914 and 1918, by some estimates, thirty-two million around the town of Verdun alone. Many did not explode but sit there still today, rusting and deadly.

Important sites on
the Western Front, 1914-18

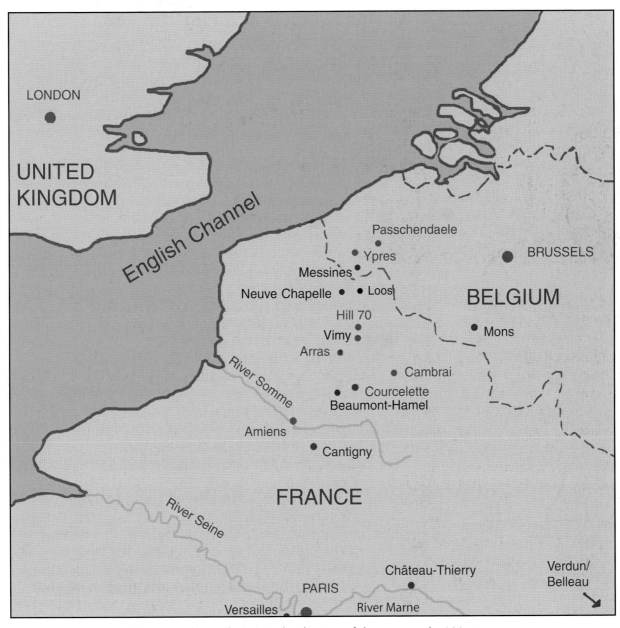

This map shows the major battle sites of the war on the Western
front in relation to the major cities of Paris and Brussels.

Timeline of World War I

1914, June 28	Franz Josef and Duchess Sophie are killed by Gavrilo Princip in Sarajevo.
1914, July 28	The Austro-Hungarian Empire declares war on Serbia.
1914, August 1	Germany declares war on Russia. Germany begins to mobilize its troops.
1914, August 3	Germany declares war on France.
1914, August 4	The United Kingdom declares war on Germany.
1914, August 23	The British see their first major action at the Battle of Mons.
1914, Aug. 17-Sept. 2	The Germans and Russians fight the Battle of Tannenberg, which the Germans win.
1914, September 5-12	The first Battle of the Marne.
1914, Oct. 31-Nov. 22	The Allies win the first battle of Ypres by holding the town.
1914, December 24	In the Christmas Truce, British, German and French troops lay down their arms for a short time.
1915, March 10	The Battle of Neuve-Chapelle
1915, April 22	The second Battle of Ypres begins. This was the first time the Germans used poison gas. This was also one of the first major engagements for Canadian soldiers.
1915, April 25	The ANZAC forces land at Gallipoli.
1915, May 7	The RMS *Lusitania* is torpedoed and sinks.
1915, August 4	The Germans capture Warsaw, Poland.
1915, September 15-28	The Battle of Loos. First British use of poison gas.
1915, September 21	Stanley Cawes is shot down and becomes Canada's first air war casualty.
1916, February 21	Germany's Verdun offensive begins. The series of battles lasts until December 16.
1916, April 29	British troops surrender at Kut, in today's Iraq.
1916, April 24	The Easter Rebellion begins in Dublin. Within a week the rebellion is crushed.
1916, May 31	The Battle of Jutland is fought off the coast of Denmark.
1916, June 4-Sept. 20	The Brusilov Offensive is a great success in driving back the German army on the Eastern Front.
1916, July 1	The Battle of the Somme begins. The British suffer 58,000 casualties that day. The results of long battle are inconclusive, as are those of many of the battles on the Western Front.
1917, January 19	The Germans send the "Zimmerman Telegram" to Mexico, which is intercepted and decoded by the British.
1917, April 6	The United States declares war on Germany.
1917, April-May	The Nivelle Offensive is a disaster for the French and triggers mutiny among the troops.
1917, April 9-12	The Battle of Vimy Ridge, part of the Battle of Arras, leads to a Canadian victory in taking the ridge.

1917, April 17	Lenin arrives in Russia, taken there with help from the Germans.
1917, April 29	French soldiers begin to mutiny.
1917, June 7-14	The Battle of Messines Ridge is an Allied victory.
1917, July 31-Nov. 06	The Battle of Passchendaele (or Third Ypres) is fought, sometimes in horrifyingly muddy conditions.
1917, November 7	Lenin's Bolsheviks storm the Winter Palace and seize control of the Russian government.
1917, November 20	Tanks are used at Cambrai to some success.
1917, December 6	The *Mont-Blanc* explodes in Halifax harbour.
1917, December 15	Russia and Germany sign an armistice.
1918, March 21	The Germans launch their massive spring offensive to try and end the war in their favour.
1918, April 21	The Red Baron is shot down.
1918, April 24	The first tank on tank battle at Villers-Bretonneux
1918, May 28	The Americans take the town of Cantigny.
1918, June 6-26	The Americans and Germans fight the Battle of Belleau Wood.
1918, July 17	The Russian royal family is executed.
1918, August 8	The Canadians attack at Amiens. It was the "black day of the German army".
1918, November 10	Canadian forces liberate Mons.
1918, November 11	Armistice is signed and the war is over.
1918, Fall	The international influenza epidemic begins.
1919, June 28	The Treaty of Versailles is signed.

Resources for learning more about World War I

The author used the following books in writing this story:

Age of Empire: 1875-1914 by E.J. Hobsbawm (New York: Vintage, 1989)

All Quiet on the Western Front by Gabriel M. Remarque
      (New York: Fawcett, 1975)

At Vimy Ridge by Hugh Brewster (Toronto: Scholastic, 2007)

Back to the Front by Stephen O'Shea (Vancouver: Douglas & McIntyre, 1997)

The First Day on the Somme by Martin Middlebrook (New York: Norton, 1972)

The First World War by Martin Gilbert (New York: Henry Holt, 1994)

The First World War by A.J.P. Taylor (London: Penguin, 1966)

The Royal Flying Corps in World War I by Ralph Banker
      (London: Robinson, 2002)

Generals Die in Bed by Charles Yale Harrison (Toronto: Annick Press, 2002)

Goodbye to All That by Robert Groves (London: Penguin, 1973)

The Kaiser's Battle by Martin Middlebrook (London: Penguin, 1983)

1914 by Lyn MacDonald (New York: Atheneum, 1987)

1915 by Lyn MacDonald (London: Headline, 1993)

Paris 1919 by Margaret MacMillan (New York: Random House, 2003)

Sagittarius Rising by Cecil Lewis (London: Penguin, 1977)

Somme by Lyn MacDonald (London: Michael Joseph, 1983)

The Penguin Book of First World War Poetry edited by Jon Silkin (London:
      Penguin, 1979)

Ten Days That Shook the World by John Reed (London: Penguin, 1977)

Tommy Goes to War by Malcolm Brown (Tempus, 1999)

Undertones of War by Edmund Blunder (London: Penguin, 1982)

Vimy by Pierre Berton (Toronto: Penguin, 1987)

Voices from the Great War by Peter Vansillant (London: Penguin, 1983)

Wilfred Owen by John Stallworthy (London: Oxford University Press, 1974)

World War I in Photographs by J.H.J Anderson (Kent: Grange Books, 2003)

World War I on the Web

There is a great deal of information about World War I on the internet. The internet changes every day. At the time that this book was printed, all of these sites were online. However, we can't guarantee that they will always be there. A simple keyword search will take you to information about the war and the history of that era.

http://www.spartacus.schoolnet.co.uk/FWW.htm
A large and very informative site

http://www.warmuseum.ca
Information about the Canadian War Museum in Gatineau, Quebec. A great place to visit for more information and to see exhibits about the war.

http://www.canadiangreatwarproject.com
A site that focusses on Canada's role and the impact of the war on the country.

http://www.firstworldwar.com
The biggest site on the war currently online. Tons of images and in-depth descriptions of battles.

http://www.worldwar1.com
Another good comprehensive site about the war from all perspectives

http://www.teacheroz.com/wwi.htm#homefront
A page with links to sites about the war in all its aspects from all over the internet

http://www.collectionscanada.ca
The Library and Archives Canada website, for in-depth information

http://www.vac-acc.gc.ca/general/sub.cfm?source=history/firstwar/canada
Veterans Affairs Canada's official World War I site

http://collectioncanada.ca/aboriginal-heritage/020016-4001-e.html
A site devoted exclusively to the role of aboriginal soldiers in the war

Index

About the author

Born in Edinburgh, Scotland, John Wilson took up writing full-time upon moving to Lantzville on Vancouver Island.

John is addicted to history and firmly believes that the past must have been just as exciting, confusing and complex to those who lived through it as our world is to us. Every one of his sixteen novels and five non-fiction books for kids, teens and adults deals with the past. His tales involve intelligent dinosaurs, angry socialist coal miners, confused boys caught up in the First and Second World Wars, and the terrors faced by lost Arctic explorers. John's most recent title, *The Alchemist's Dream*, was shortlisted for the Governor General's Award.

John has also written the *Weet* fiction series for Napoleon, as well as the Stories of Canada titles *Righting Wrongs: The Story of Norman Bethune* and *Discovering the Arctic: The Story of John Rae*. Both were shortlisted for the Norma Fleck Award for children's non-fiction.

Stories of Canada
by John Wilson

Righting Wrongs: The Story of Norman Bethune
Discovering the Arctic: The Story of John Rae

Photo and Art Credits